LIPSTICK

JESSICA PALLINGSTON

●

ST. MARTIN'S PRESS
NEW YORK

FOR JOHN BLAKE

Interior Illustrations pp 58–59 by Meryl Gross

Book design by Maura Fadden Rosenthal/Mspace

Library of Congress Cataloging-in-Publication Data
Pallingston, Jessica.
    Lipstick / by Jessica Pallingston.—1st ed.
      p.   cm.
    Includes bibliographical references.
    ISBN 0-312-19914-7
    1. Lipstick.   I. Title.
   GT2340.P35   1999
   391.6'3—dc21   98-27749
                                        CIP

ISBN 0-312-19914-7

First Edition: January 1999

10 9 8 7 6 5 4 3 2 1

"Hand me my purse, will you, darling?
A girl can't read that sort of thing without
her lipstick."

CONTENTS

Studies have shown that women
who wear red lipstick
smile more

INTRODUCTION

CONFESSIONS OF A LIPSTICK ADDICT

I don't know how or when it started.

I only know that now I am an addict. A full-fledged, all-the-way, no-turning-back addict. Hooked. A junkie.

I must have lipstick amnesia, though, because every time I try to think back into the past, and figure out how my obsession started, my memory gets fuzzy—sort of that color you get when you mix Frostwave Brown and Glitter Night.

But the addiction has become fierce. The rules of the addiction are complex and arduous: Must have it on when I leave the house. Must wear it when I'm in the house.

Must carry at least five tubes with me at all times. Must have at least one matte, one gloss, and one scented lipstick at all times. Must be wearing it when I go to sleep. Must wear it when driving a car. Must change lipstick color at least four times a day. Must wear darker colors when nervous. Must have emergency lipstick in car glove compartment.

And I know I'm not alone on some of this. There are others out there. Lots of them.

How else do you attest for some of these statistics?

It is estimated that 75–85% of all American women wear lipstick. Lipstick sales often outnumber other cosmetic products four to one. Clinique alone sells one every second during their retail operation.

Most lipstick addicts confess to carrying their lipsticks as religiously as they carry wallets and keys. Actually, some say they've left the house forgetting their wallets and their keys—but not their lipstick. Addicts confess to stealing it from drugstores in junior high, as if they were under a spell when they did it; and these are girls who otherwise didn't even know how to steal. Then there are those women who used to hide it from their parents, like they were stashing drugs in their purse. If they got caught, maybe even punished, it didn't matter—they were back at it in seconds.

What is it about lipstick?

There's something about the way it looks and feels. There's a ritual to putting it on. It's a bite-sized magic wand. All my years of oral fixation seem to have found a compassionate partner in lipstick. It's like a drug. An instant fix for sex appeal and glamour.

It appears on the counters of drug and department stores with the come-hither wink of candy and chocolate. As soon as I'm in a store, I subconsciously gravitate toward the lipstick counter. I don't know what it is. Maybe it's those colors. And if I'm feeling slightly depressed, forget it. In two seconds, I'm trying on every bullet I can get my hands on. I think I've put the children of a few makeup-counter ladies through college.

Over the years, I've amassed over 100 tubes of the stuff. I can usually tell someone the name of the color and the brand that they are wearing. I can tell the brand of a lipstick with my eyes shut, just by its scent. I'm waiting for the day that I can tell the color with my eyes shut, too.

I can usually spot another junkie within the first ten minutes of conversation.

The confessions of the lipstick addicts are a world unto themselves. They talk about lipstick as if these things were not just tubes of colored wax. Oh, no. They talk about lipstick as if it were a part of them—an appendage or something. It marks their identity. Lipstick is a way for a woman to mark her territory. A lipstick print on a glass or a collar is an alluring, mysterious, sometimes ominous step up from "Kilroy Was Here."

My friend Betty insists her lipsticks are charms. "My mother told me the only real way to catch a man is with red lipstick. Pink will scare them away, orange will make them nauseous. Red casts the spell."

Apparently, lipstick is taken seriously in Betty's house. Almost a form of suburban witchcraft.

My friend Maude, who grew up in 1960s London, recalls getting into big trouble when her father found her tube of Innoxa lipstick called "Postman's Knock." Sent to her room without dinner, not allowed to leave the house for a week. This made the sixteen-year-old even more sure of what could and would happen if she let that red candy roll across her lips.

Sometimes lipstick junkies talk about their lipsticks as if they were weapons—an essential weapon in the ritual of creating the artifice that's necessary to be female.

A key player in the never ending (and never completely achievable) quest and hunt for feminity. I can just imagine the cavegirls wandering through the wastelands of the past, out on the hunt. Surely they must have been wearing lipstick.

Assuredly the long tip of the lipstick wand must reach way back into the dawn of man, if not the dawn of the unconscious. Today, a woman puts on lipstick before leaving her urban or suburban cave. That red slice of wax is the passport that takes her from her unseen, protected, private self to the arena of the visible, unprotected, public self. With that gash on her mouth, she is able to enter into combat with the outside world. Just like a cavegirl, really— who painted an outdoor self onto the body in order to battle the mysterious world beyond her skin. A few stripes of red on the cheek or lips would protect against the devil. I often feel this way when I put on my face for work.

I say lipstick is a primal need. There's something about lipstick a girl can't help but be attracted to. It's a combination of primitive need and a magic wand. I do know one thing: It is through lipstick that I feel a bond with the lone woman huddled in the cave a couple million years ago, smearing red dye on her lips. It's a pretty extraordinary connection.

And so, for all the cavegirls of yesteryear, and all the girls who can't help it today, here is my valentine to history's favorite cosmetic.

CHAPTER ONE

A BRIEF HISTORY OF LIPSTICK

What is lipstick anyway?

The sad truth—it's not much more than a mixture of wax, oil, and color.

Throughout history, skincare potions have gone from puppy-dog-fat wrinkle creams and splashing on one's own urine in the sixteenth century, to mixtures of pig brain, alligator intestine, and wolf blood in the Middle Ages (finding the stuff was your own problem). But lipstick has been remarkably well behaved, and the ingredients have pretty much stayed the same.

Until the twentieth century, cosmetics were usually

concocted at home, lipcolor included. In making these potions in home labs, there were reports of poisoning (and a few explosions). The gentle home could take on toxic proportions. Most likely, a large amount of these hack pharmacists never reported their mishaps to either the authorities or their families.

For most of history, lipcolor was made from paste, and referred to as lip paint or lip rouge, and has most often been available in a pot. Women possessed their "pots of rouge"—some for cheeks, and some for lips. The wealthier the woman, the more pots to her name.

It was during World War I when lipstick was reinvented in bullet form and given its new name—the brainchild of a laboratory engineer who must surely have been inspired and influenced to some extent by the ammunition plants, and the new league of women factory laborers at work.

But let's go back to the dawn of the lipstick. . . .

The first lipstick was found in the Sumerian region of Ur, and was estimated to be 5,000 years old. Ur is roughly 200 miles south of Babylon. This is where our Bible pal Abraham was living with his people when he was called by the voice of God to set out and find a new land.

It's not surprising that this is the site of the first lipstick. Sumer is a hot spot for historical firsts: first schools, first case of juvenile delinquency, first farmer's almanac, first love story, first lullaby, first tax cut, first "sick society."[1]

But like so much else, lipstick soon fell prey to the Dark Ages.

But before there was a Dark Age, there was a Golden Age. And the first Golden Age can be found among the same people who created one of the other great totems to feminine mystique: the Sphinx.

THE FIRST GOLDEN AGE OF LIPSTICK— ANCIENT EGYPT: An Egyptian woman owned a brass or wooden makeup kit filled with little pots in which to mix colors—like the best makeup artists today. The kit included perfume, egg whites (for facials), pumice stones and razors (to scrape off body hair, which was considered the ultimate in grossness), crushed ant eggs for kohl, mortar and pestles to grind, henna for nails and hands, plant stems filled with colored dyes for eye makeup and lip rouge, and slimy ointments for that very hip accessory— lip gloss. Although ancient Egypt was really first and foremost the Golden Age of eye makeup, it was during this epoch that lipstick art and technique as we now know it was established. And although lips did take a backseat to the eyes, the Egyptians were no slouches in the lipstick department. They were masters at mixing color, precise application, and glamorous packaging.

Egyptians favored blue-black lipstick, with the second runners-up being orange and a reddish magenta (painted on with a wet stick of wood). A fashionable man also painted his lips. It was important for the chic Egyptian to always look his or her best. After all, you never knew who you might meet. Or you could find yourself meeting death at any time. For this possibility the Egyptian woman was doubly prepared—she always went well stocked into the afterlife, making sure she had two pots of rouge buried with her in her tomb.

THE LIPS OF ANCIENT GREECE: Ancient Greece was good for the boys, not for the girls. Women were expected to stay at home and rarely allowed out in public.

The good Greek housewife was like an ancient version of June Cleaver or Donna Reed. Her liprouge was elegant and tasteful, made from red dyes and strong wines. Some cosmetic ingredients included sheep sweat, human saliva, and crocodile excrement—but even sweat and excrement were to be used with restrained elegance and taste. The real pleasure of gaudy and advanced lipcoloring was reserved for another sector of society: prostitutes. Ancient Greece may not have been a Golden Age of lipstick, but it was *the* Golden Age of prostitution. We may have supermodels today, but this was the age of the super-prostitutes. These girls had all the fun—sloshing on white lead powder, caking on colors, and having more fun with lipstick than even Boy George. However, the bad babes of antiquity did have some strict and intricate rules of order—there are cases of some prostitutes appearing publicly at the wrong time, minus their designated slut gear or trampy face, then punished for improperly posing as ladies, perhaps the first known incidents of unlawful drag in reverse.

ANCIENT ROME AND THE WONDERFUL WORLD OF MAKEUP SLAVES: The Roman housewife had it a little better. Not a lot better, but a little. Poppaea, the crazy wife of the crazy emperor Nero, imposed her nutty standards for beauty onto the masses. She had no less than 100 attendants to maintain her looks, and engaged in bizarre beauty rituals round the clock, religiously keeping her lips painted. A reddish purple mercuric plant dye called fucus (little did Poppaea or anyone else know it was a potentially deadly poison) and sediments from red wine were sold at the market for use in liprouge. Like Poppaea, most Roman women had their very own makeup and hairstyling slaves at home, and it was not uncommon for the unhappy housewife to whip the hell out of her slave if she was dissatisfied with the result of her lipstick or hairdo. Men also wore the stuff, with some colors indicating social standing and rank. To harmonize with her fucus- and wine-colored lips, the Roman lady added a unibrow and a blond wig—only the best of which were ripped off the heads of barbarians and brought back from battle by her old man.

LIPSTICK SLIDES INTO THE DARK AGES: Damn barbarians, once they showed up, all lipcolor advancements of the previous Golden Age end up being for nothing. Lipstick, like so much else, got thrown into the wide abyss of darkness. The in-vogue barbarian man wore a blue face and blue lips when charging into battle, in order to scare the enemy. That enemy was usually wearing his own colors to do some scaring back. Along with their makeup, hair also took on terrorist duties—often dyed a vicious punk red or a deranged blue.

Back at home, while the men were off on their Halloween battlefields, barbarianettes were no better off. Always a sign of an age suffering from glamour malnourishment is lipstick neglect. The toilet of the mouth was given scant attention. Barb women spent most of their allotted vanity time on *hair* products, concocting what they assumed to be very posh creams, made of lizard fat and bird droppings. Barbarian pop culture was far too obsessed with hair and fur, which, in my opinion, was the cause of their eventual downfall.

MEDIEVAL MAKEUP: This is one of my favorite periods of lipstick history because it is so screwed up. The medieval zeitgeist embraced a fear of living and a passion for the afterlife. It was now chic to look dead. The body was seen as an evil that only made you want to have sex, thereby raising the stakes for your chances of going to hell. Ears were condemned as sexy body parts by the church (reason: Mary gave birth to Jesus through her ear), and were thus almost always covered. A woman who wore makeup was seen as an incarnation of Satan. After all, taking over and redoing the face surely must be a way of challenging God. "How dare you think you could do a better job than He?" was a common line in the writing of the saints. And furthermore, as Saint Jerome said, if a rouged woman looked up at God on Judgment Day, there was no way he'd be able to recognize her. Medieval paintings depicting hell showed vain babies having beauty rituals performed on them by the Devil himself. Example: Hair plucked out with hot, mordantly painful tweezers.

This was the era of Lipstick as Satan.

Women brave or beauty-obsessed enough to defy God could obtain that In look—Le Morte Chic—by smearing their skin with flour, bathing in ass' milk, and avoiding fresh air (which all glam women knew ruined the complexion). Lipcolor could be used to make the skin look whiter. The few beauty scribes who managed to surface and survive advised making the face the color of the lily and the lips the color of the rose. As long as you explained your makeup as being the lily/rose thing, you could get away with it, under the guise of being poetic. This rose lip shmear was a concoction of sheep fat and smashed up red roots. The look was then completed with a face 100 percent freed of hair—by way of quicklime and pincers, and a forehead high enough to serve a meal on.

THE SECOND GOLDEN AGE OF LIPSTICK or DID ELIZABETH ARDEN GET HER NAME FROM ELIZABETH TUDOR? Lipstick had its next Golden Age in the reign of that half-masculine/ half-feminine queen, Elizabeth. Forget for a moment about Estèe Lauder, Helena Rubinstein, and other great madames of makeup and commerce. The first true beauty tycoon was Liz I. The Renaissance, with its newfound love of all that was earthly, fueled makeup's comeback. Given Liz's obsession with the stuff, makeup was accorded a new respect and value. During her reign, makeup was sometimes used as a substitute for cash in trade. Cosmetic vendors appeared on the street, and everyone tried to recreate Liz's face on their own (warning: if you were of the poorer classes, and did so, it was cause for arrest). The In Look was still white skin, but now with more vibrant colors on the lips, eyes, and cheeks.

Accounts of the paint-loving Elizabeth's fight against her own death are thick with lipstick and powder. Determined to stay alive, she applied coat upon coat of makeup to her face. Some reports say that when she died, Elizabeth had close to a half inch of lipstick on. But then, this would make sense, since makeup vendors were considered to be part magician. The liprouge and other concoctions these hawkers sold were whispered to be miracle potions that could work magic—maybe even against death.

THE THIRD GOLDEN AGE OF LIPSTICK— THE BAROQUE: From 1660–1789, the French and the Brits really went overboard with the lipstick thing. At times, it would have looked to our contemporary eye like a society ruled by drag queens. This was *the* Golden Age of liprouge for men, and every respectable male member of society wore the stuff. An all-purpose fashion and lipstick dictator was found in Marie Antoinette, who carved out the rules for the perfect mouth: round and pearl-like, with just the right combo of plump and slender. You never saw any big, puffy bee-stung lips among the In Crowd. No, only the peasant class had those, God forbid.

Madame de Pompadour, mistress to King Louis XV, expanded the art of Looking Beautiful to a full-time job, complete with overtime and benefits. The all-consuming hours she spent in creating the perfectly proportioned and colored face, as well as the 100 percent perfect blend of *au naturale* and artifice is said to have killed her—she died from exhaustion.

Lipstick's purpose was to get attention in a crowd. Considering the fact that heads were topped with sky-high wigs and a barrage of colored patches adorned people's faces, standing out took some work. Newspapers warned naive travelers en route to Paris to beware—the shock of this surreal artifice could stop a human heart. Translation: Tourism could be a form of death.

EIGHTEENTH-CENTURY AMERICANS HIPPIES? or JUST ANOTHER ARM OF THE ESTABLISHMENT, MAN?

The Americans are often depicted as the hippies of the Baroque—going barefaced and *au naturale*. After all, Benjamin Franklin became a fashion-rebel sensation in France when he pranced around in his Ben Frankliny brand of hippy chic: straggly hair, John Lennon glasses, and frumpy clothes. But don't be fooled.

There was some great face paint to be found in the New World. The colonists saw it on the Indians' skin. Some European courts imitated the New World Indians—complete with Mohawk haircuts and face painting. Soon, many of the fashion-obsessed back home in Europe were buying one-way tickets for American-bound ships. There was money to be made off the riches and resources abroad.

The colonial men were worse than the women. The male colonist started the day by taking a seat before the mirror for his daily toilet. Virginians were the worst. Strips of bacon were slapped onto their cheeks at night for a soft, pink skin, and in the morning, Spanish Papers of Rouge (papers thickened with carmine dye) were rubbed on for color. One popular rouging agent was Bavarian Red Liquor. There were two ways you could use it: rub it on, or drink it down. Either way, a rosy glow was promised. For the more thrifty, there was yet another lipstick option: carrying lemons in the pocket, to be sucked on throughout the day to give lips a real zinger redness.

For the Puritan settlers, however, rouging the lips was *not* a cool thing to do. The more daring women would rub snips of red ribbon onto their mouths when no one was looking. This practice set a nice foundation for the paranoid and slightly delusional attitude toward lipstick that would characterize much of the nineteenth century.

NINETEENTH-CENTURY NERVOUS BREAK-DOWN: For a good part of the 1800s, makeup was for tramps and actors, period. Such was the sentiment set by Queen Victoria, who publicly declared that makeup was impolite. A beauty expert for the *Saturday Evening Review* in 1854 threw in her own two cents, denouncing makeup as insincere and a form of lying. Paint was for sinful actresses, like Sarah Bernhardt. Sarah was an extreme example, however. She really took it too far when she actually applied liprouge *in public* (God forbid, the hussy), causing one of the biggest scandals of the time.

But the makeup that actors used was rank, primitive stuff. Mascara came in hard cake form and had to be heated by flame into a liquid, then quickly applied before it dried up again. Lip and cheek rouge were made by mixing pigmented powder with butter or lard (butter for the more skin-conscious actress), and once again a candle had to be kept handy to keep the mixtures from congealing.

Paleness continued to be the vogue. In the early part of the century, tuberculosis took on the same allure that heroin chic did in the 1990s. Lord Byron rhapsodized a bit too eloquently on TB, and soon it was cool to look sick—something of a throwback to medieval chic—but now it was dying, rather than actually being dead, that was considered glamorous. To get this sickly romantic look, women drank vinegar and arsenic. Belladonna, a poisonous liquid, was dropped in the eyes. This not only dilated the pupils for a dreamy and misty look, it also had the bonus side effect of causing hallucinations.

Thus, for part of the century, death and madness became a routine part of making up.

As the nineteenth century continued on to the later stages of its nervous breakdown, products were sold that would melt flesh (the popular term for losing weight) as you sat in the bathtub; rubber ear and nose flatteners hit the shops; and recipes surfaced for melting down double chins and big lips.

But cosmetics were viewed more and more as taboo and were forced to go through the end of the century in drag as medicine. Beauty came from within, period. And the medical makeup quack found a new home on the edge of the medicine profession.

The lipstick business by and large went underground, into a bootlegging wasteland of amateur pharmacist-cooks, or anyone with a knack for mixing potions. Liprouge was spoken of aboveground as *the* most indecent of all makeup, and the lipstick societies underground traded recipes as if they were cooking up moonshine.

THE TWENTIETH CENTURY, AGE OF THE FOX: Slowly, lipstick came out of exile. And once it did, it really took off.

At the turn of the century, the French company Guerlain introduced liprouge in stick form, making what some attribute as perhaps the first public appearance of the product beyond the walls of the theater and onto the shelves of posh shops.

The first modern lipsticks in a metal case were produced by Maurice Levy and the Scovil Manufacturing Company of Waterbury, Connecticut, in 1915, right smack in the middle of World War I. While the Guerlain products were available to a limited aristocratic clientele, the new Scovil metal-tubed lipsticks were available to the masses, and became immediately popular with the new force of working women.

The same year that the metal-tubed lipsticks came into the world, the parasol passed into oblivion. By 1910, the *Sears Catalog* stopped peddling products that promised "beauty from within" and focused instead on beauty being applied and obtained from the outside.

Lipstick became a symbol of women's lib. In a form of inverse feminism, Elizabeth Cady Stanton, Charlotte Perkins Gilman, and other notable feminists marched at the front of a 1912 NYC Suffragette rally, all wearing painted lips as a badge of emancipation.

Urban decay was another reason for lipstick's reentry into society. As the century turned, cities grew. Factories sprouted up faster; pollution spread. Face paint was needed—if for nothing else as a mask. In toiletry ads, the mouth was increasingly depicted as an innocent little hole, unwittingly sucking in germs. Magazines gallantly offered products that would protect the poor little mouth from the big bad world beyond the face.

1920s: LIKE THE WOMEN WHO WEAR IT, LIPSTICK COMES INTO ITS OWN: With the labors of invention done for them in the 1910s, the 1920s got to have the real fun with lipstick. Where once upon a time a fashion dictator was found in Marie Antoinette, now the dictator was found in the flickering images of celluloid.

Film, the great new art, was particularly good for lipstick. Almost every lip color and shape was advertised via the image of a particular movie star. Magazines peddled such standard commodities as the Clara Bow Look, the Theda Bara Look, or the Mae Murray Look. Lips became as easy as paint by number, with the mouths of the stars as outlines. Clara had the "Cupid's Bow," Theda the "Vamp Lips," and for Mae it was the "Bee-stung Lips." The various lip shapes, from vampire to rosebud, were the beeswax personifiers of carefree, evil, or virginal characters, and were copied by women watching from the audience.

The popular Bee-stung Mouth actually came about as a way to solve a movie lighting problem, and the problem solver was Max Factor. The hot lamps of the studio caused lip pomade to run, so Max placed a greasepaint foundation around the mouth to cover its natural outlines, then pressed two thumb prints of pomade onto the upper lip, and two upside-down thumbprints on the bottom. He then took a brush to draw in the lip corners and contours. He used black, since red and pink had a rather funky effect when photographed.[2]

These silver-screen mouths, drawn in daring styles, and constantly pursuing romantic actions, created a new interest in the kiss. Every accessory a kiss might need was now on sale: mirrored lipstick containers, flavored lipsticks, garnet- and black-colored lipsticks (to look like they did on screen), lip tracers and self-shaping lipsticks to assist in drawing a Cupid's Bow. Maybelline made "kissproof" lipstick. A barbaric-looking mechanical steel device was patented in 1924 by an enterprising engineer, to be worn on the upper lip like a clamp, in order to swell the mouth and shape it into a puffy pout.

Cosmetics became the fourth largest industry in

America (after automobiles, movies, and bootlegging liquor), and within that industry, lipstick was the favorite product. By 1929, Elizabeth Arden was as much a household name as Coca Cola and Singer Sewing Machines. Once considered a vulgar act, painting one's lips in public was now the bee's knees of stylish behavior. Max Factor decided to name his products *make-up* instead of *cosmetics* (*make-up* was previously only the term for theater products), and other companies jumped on the boat. *Actress, show biz,* and *makeup,* once ugly words, were now associated with the height of glamour.

However, like so much that is fashionable, lipstick was not exactly comfortable. The twenties lipstick could be impossibly matte and thick. After all, it was made with a soap base.

THE SMILE OF THE DEPRESSION—THE 1930s: There was a severity to the thirties look, as if austerity was actually painted onto the face. Angular sharp edges defined the decade, with Dietrich and Garbo offering another paint-by-number standard. The face was hard and cynical, as a face should be after seeing the Roaring Twenties collapse into depression. Makeup went from a seductive and flirtatious look to one of "perfection," perhaps a subliminal attempt at perfecting a very imperfect world. While women had previously found a new emancipation in having their own jobs and money in the twenties, now it was a fast jump back to the old days. A restrictive style in fashion quickly returned.

"Face shapers" and "lip stencils" were hot items. Technical tips from the movies crammed the beauty magazines. Slices of colored cellophane film, to be worn once and then discarded, appeared as testers. The fashion was a severe mouth, outlined with the new product: lipliner.

So that consumers felt they were saving money, companies combined separate makeup into one product—perfume was now added to lipstick.

Helena Rubinstein ran the first clinical lipstick ads, featuring sun protectants. With the advent of Technicolor, women could not only shop by screen for the shape of their lips, but for the color as well. Lipcolor and shades expanded, including the full-blast colors of Elsa Schiaparelli's lipstick—"Schiap," a bright yellowish pink and "Shocking," a hot fuchsia. Beauty salons opened everywhere, providing a sanctuary from the bleak world in the same way the escapist, lavish movie musicals did. Makeup was one of the few industries that came out of the Depression wealthier than when it went in. As Elizabeth Arden said: "The more they chew their fingernails, wrinkle their brows, and pull their hair, the more they need us." However destitute, people still found money to spend on beauty and entertainment—movies and lipstick.[3]

But the child-woman of the 1920s grew up when the hard reality of the thirties set in. If the turn of the century was the birth of the era, the 1910s the training wheels for the new millennium, and the twenties its adolescence, the thirties were its transition into adulthood. In the thirties one thing became clear: Lipstick was here to stay.

THE 1940s—WAR PAINT FOR CIVILIANS AND KISSING MACHINES: Women learned how to fight war at home by making up. Putting on powder and lipstick was a form of morale boosting. It was keeping up a good face. It was the duty of every female citizen. Tangee (one of the biggest lipstick companies of the era) launched a "War, Women, and Lipstick" campaign: "If a symbol were needed of this fine, independent spirit—of this courage and strength—I would choose a lipstick. It is one of those mysterious little essentials that have an importance far beyond their size or cost. A woman's lipstick is an instrument of personal morale that helps her to conceal heartbreak or sorrow; gives her self confidence when it's badly needed . . . No lipstick, ours or anyone else's, will win the war. But it symbolizes one of the reasons why we are fighting—the precious right of women to be feminine and lovely under any circumstances."

Women horded their lipsticks. Ads begged women to please buy sparingly, and to save their lipstick for nights out only. In a prominent article written after World War II, lipstick was cited as the "most missed" among the shortages of war. Nurses evacuated by submarines escaped clutching only a few items—but always their lipsticks.

An editorial in a 1941 *Vogue* magazine asked the question: "Is it patriotic to worry about my looks at a time like this?" A soldier answered for *Vogue*: "To look unattractive these days is downright morale-breaking and should be considered treason." So it was that a lipsticked American woman was a good American. The feds conducted tests and surveys on morale. Their finding: Makeup was an effective morale builder and helped ease combat fatigue. The U.S. Director of Economic Stabilization ordered factory dressing rooms to be stocked with lipstick to improve efficiency. The British government, on the other hand, didn't buy the idea. Lipstick production ceased in their country, and a black market of lipstick bootleggers flourished in the war-torn streets of London.

THE '50s: WAR ENDS AND LIPSTICK DOES ITS PART FOR REPOPULATION: War was over, and society's subconscious turned to reproduction. It was the age of Marilyn Monroe and Jayne Mansfield, of Christian Dior's "New Look" dress that cinched the waist and pushed out those maternal breasts and childbearing hips. Makeup emphasized the lips, painted bright red or plum. The pouty and childish mouth of Marilyn Monroe became the stamp of the decade ("I am constantly running into people's unconscious," she said). The forever fighting Bette Davis and Joan Crawford had a duel of the lips: Who could be more over-the-top? Both stars dramatically reshaped their lips with lipstick to fit the era's new look—painting them beyond the normal, natural line of the mouth. Lips were made to seem fuller, healthier, and more seductive. The angular lips of the previous age were out. It was time to reproduce again. The word "teenager" arrived as an everyday word, and with this newly discovered consumer group, lipstick marketing would never be the same. Perhaps not unrelated to this fact was the intensified interest in the gamine, quickly personified in Audrey Hepburn. The image of the "girl" made its way into all avenues of commerce. New lipsticks appeared that targeted teens. The decade's hot-selling lipsticks, with girlish names like "Milkmaid Pink," were sold on drugstore shelves side by side with the dime novels—among them, another gamine-as-subject best-seller, *Lolita.*

BABY-FACED OUTER SPACE ANDROGYNES or THE 1960s LIPSTICK: Makeup took inspiration from men walking on the moon, and lipstick went 2001 with pale zombie colors and space-age silvers. The popular image was the Innocent, lauded in the anorexic-adolescent-chic of nineteen-year-old Twiggy. Some feminists complained that lipstick was now made with, or simulated, the same ingredients used in products for infants and toddlers—such as baby powder, baby oil, bubble bath, and cotton candy. White and pearly beige became big sellers. Women still wanted to wear lipstick, but they wanted to wear lipstick that made them look like they weren't wearing lipstick. To achieve this, the most complicated and difficult formulas in lipstick history were concocted. Fish scales were used to make glittery, frosted covers. Mary Quant, a player in the burgeoning Pop Art scene, and a major innovator in sixties makeup, made snide comments about the usual array of pinks, then created her own pale and shiny takes on the old standby. Quant introduced pots of gloss, as well as a half-and-half lipstick, called Skitzo. Art and fashion became closer cousins in the 1960s. Quant came out with the "Paint Box," stocked with pencils, brushes, pastel shadows, and an instruction book in the style of a painter's guide. Andy Warhol also influenced fashion (and in turn, lipstick color and style) with his plastic, reflective, and glittery silver images, which he described as evocative of a trance and outer space. The popular product Erase, previously used only as a concealer, was now used on the lips. Erase did exactly what its name promised—it got rid of the mouth, but still allowed it to be painted, and switched the focus back up to eye makeup, which was enjoying its biggest golden age since Cleopatra.

THE '70s TO THE '90s:

> "First there's disco, then there's punk, then there's lipstick that's named Gunk. First there's purple, then there's black, then there's lipstick that's called Crap."
>
> —ANONYMOUS

There's the Edwardian Era, the Victorian Era, and Georgian Era, all named for Englishmen on the throne. The seventies to the nineties were periods where the man on the Washington throne cast his shadow across the nations—and perhaps the colors of these shadows affected the pigment choice in lipstick. There was the Ronaldian era, the Dickian, Jimmian, Bushian, and Billian, all reflecting colors back: "Gashlit Purple," "Marvelous Darkness," "Surprise Nude," "Barely There," "Secrecy Red," and "Dead-end Black."

THE 1970s: Disco made its mark on lipstick, anointing purple as the decade's reigning color. As the seventies inched along, black became the color of choice for the punk population, very nicely expressing sex and violence. And the New Agers eased their way into the market, too—natural plant- and cell-extract bases started showing up in lipstick ingredients. Yves Saint Laurent introduced his lipstick line. This was one of the first times colors appeared that were marked not with names but numbers. The most popular in Yves' line was a pure fuchsia, otherwise known as Number 19.

The real trendsetters in lipstick came through rock 'n' roll. The band the New York Dolls (sometimes referred to as "anarchy in lipstick"), took the stage in heavy makeup, used a fuschia lipstick drawing out their name as their logo, and are often credited as getting the lipstick ball rolling in rock. Now it was the *guys,* however, who were doing the lipstick trendsetting: David Bowie, Gary Glitter, Kiss, Alice Cooper, and a newly lipsticked Mick Jagger.[4]

WHEN THE EIGHTIES CREPT IN, PUNK WAS STILL WRITHING ON THE STREETS OF THE CITY: Critics compared the pale faces and blackened lips to the ravaged look of the sick during a plague. Later, it was noted by some pop culture writers that lipstick was a silent prophet to the new plague lurking silently within society, about to show its face: AIDS.

Colors got darker, lips got wider. Getting lip collagen injections became, for some women, as normal as going to the dentist. Lipstick role models came via TV stars with big hair and shoulder pads, as well as the halloween/transvestite chic of Boy George. Make-up companies gave their lipsticks names that sounded like the names of rock bands, and made them in the colors of Punk, Heavy Metal, and Disco.

THE NINETIES SAW A LIPSTICK RENAISSANCE as new makeup companies emerged at a rapid pace, most of them emphasizing their lipsticks. Fashion mags peddled a bare face wearing only lipstick in an off-kilter color. Many new companies were the dream children of makeup artists—a formerly unexploited subsector of celebrity. Two houses created lipstick specifically for Madonna. New kid on the block, Urban Decay, was sued by Mattel for using the name Barbie, alongside some Quant-like comments about pink being like puke. Urban Decay also created lip products named Gunk, Gash, and Roach, and other very non-Barbie names.

M•A•C hired the openly lesbian singer kd lang and drag queen RuPaul as spokespeople. Gothic rock and shock rockers joined the lipstick landscape with black, blue, and other shockingly colored lips. A coffee culture fad took off, and browns popped up in almost everyone's lipstick line. Estèe Lauder created Coffee Bar Lipsticks. The popularity of the color brown (often associated as a symbol of penance) got further notice in makeup and fashion, and was written of as possibly being one way that Americans were paying penance for the decadence of the eighties. Other attempts at stoic religiousness in fashion were showcased in Jean Paul Gaultier's Hasidic Jew collection and Isaac Mizrahi's Pilgrim look.

At the end of the decade, politically correct lipstick became most important. Companies made makeup that resembled at-home alchemy kits, in which you could induce your own do-it-yourself bliss, calm, or serenity.

Makeup often touted vitamin and herbal ingredients, and lipstick was pictured in magazine editorials as chopped up and curled pieces of color, looking like ground herbs and spices.

Ancient forms of magic continued to be recycled via the lipstick.

Hemp resurfaced in its industrial form, promising to provide supreme moisturizing qualities. And even though this form of hemp contained no drugs, the idea of lipstick to get you high or mellow you out was subconsciously suggested.

St. John's Wort, used to free the air of devils during the Middle Ages, and which the new decade saw as a form of Prozac Lite, found its way into lipstick.

More ancient forms of magic can be expected to be pulled from the attic, to be revamped through lipstick—promising newer, better, and bigger forms of enchantment via the wax and the tube.

And with that, lipstick takes off into the twenty-first century.

CHAPTER TWO

LIPSTICK FOR BEGINNERS

Lipstick Explained:
The Top Egghead Theories

"I guess I've always been fascinated with lipstick because of its candylike appearance. I remember climbing onto our bathroom counter and opening the medicine chest in search of my mom's orange lipstick. Since smells can be deceiving (her tube had a distinct floral scent), I naturally decided to have a bite. The waxy texture yielded not a single iota of orange taste. After spitting out all but what had melted between my teeth, I quickly set about reshaping what was left to her liprouge. Not realizing quite how delicate the bullet of color was, I suddenly found myself holding the lipstick and container in different hands. I wish I had a picture of me as my mother entered the bathroom to find everything in sight colored coral. I've learned a lot about lipstick since then."

— MAKEUP ARTIST KEVYN ACOIN,
FROM *Making Faces*

25

Some of us are still mystified. Lipstick is like a black hole. Or ice cream.

Black holes are too mystifying to understand. Ice cream too, if you ask me. Anybody who knows chocolate ice cream knows it's not *just chocolate*. Its therapeutic and emotional values go much further, hitting much deeper nerves and senses. And lipstick is not *just* a *cosmetic*. It's like makeup's mysterious cousin who happens to be a witch. We're not talking namby-pamby powder here. There's more to lipstick than that.

There is something about making lipstick that incorporates the quest to capture the perfect secret ingredients, to make the perfect product, the ultimate, sublime creation. Evidence: The industry war that broke out over lipstick in the 1950s. For about ten years, the companies nearly destroyed one another in an attempt to find the secrets of the perfect lipstick.

Reports came that thugs were being sent into stores to destroy the competitors' displays. Everyone was accused of stealing formulas and marketing secrets from everyone else. Companies had the telephones of their own staff members bugged. Hazel Bishop (inventor of the modern lanolin lipstick) accused the Toni Company of theft. As she did this, Revlon ripped off Hazel. Coty sued Revlon for stolen ad copy. In 1955, the New York State Joint Legislative Committee met to study the "illegal interception of communications." Revlon used *The $64,000 Dollar Question* to hawk their products, then was accused of rigging their show, and contestants were brought forward to confess. Lawsuits, paranoia, suspicion, theft, phone tapping, crime. All this for lipstick? A tube of wax in a metal flask?

Lipstick couldn't be that big a deal, could it?

Why do we wear it anyhow? What's its purpose? How can it be explained?

What follows are the top fourteen theories, as proposed by various lipstick eggheads.

THEORY #1: THE GIRL CAN'T HELP IT

"According to anthropologists, the lips remind us of the labia, because they flush red and swell when aroused, which is the conscious or subconscious reason women have always made them look even redder with lipstick," writes Diane Ackerman in *A Natural History of the Senses*.

Animal behaviorist Desmond Morris doesn't stop with just the lipstick. He gives each item of makeup its due in this popular theory: Eye makeup is used to give the glassy-eyed look, and blush to get the flushed skin of orgasm. Fashion sociologist Julian Robinson agrees. In his book *Body Packaging,* Robinson writes that "the human body undergoes physiological changes when sexually aroused, and the real appeal of such aids as cosmetics and perfumes is that they mimic these changes. . . . The eyelids become more colorful. Lips redden, cheeks and earlobes blush."

Does this mean that we are all walking around trying to simulate a nonstop orgasm?

Maybe.

The sociologist Flugel adds his two cents to the pot: "Among savage peoples, clothing and decoration . . . start anatomically at or near the genital region and have very frequently some definite reference to a sexual occasion." So, body decoration starts at the sex organs and moves outward. Once again, lipstick has its routes down below.

John X, the egghead who lives in my neighborhood, explains further:

"Lipstick implies 'I've done it,' or 'I do it.' If a woman wears lipstick when talking to a man, what she's saying is,

'This conversation could definitely lead to sex.' Lipstick is an affirmation of your sexuality. That's why it's sort of touching when you see older women wearing lipstick. It is a monument or reminder of sexuality that's gone. Rather than being an active vehicle of attraction, it is a poignant reminder of something lost. Usually a virgin will wear pink. When she crosses over to the I-Did-It camp, she'll start wearing red. A lot of girls tell you they won't wear red, only pink, but if you ask them why, they're not really sure. They'll say, 'Oh, the color isn't right,' or 'I'm too young for that much color.' I can tell you why, though."

THEORY #2: MOUTHOLOGY

When you're born, a long life of mouth enslavement begins. This is where lipstick training begins. From infancy, it's the key connector to the world beyond one's own skin.

For primates, especially humans, most of their outside world contact is through the eyes, nose, and mouth. It is precisely this that makes them different from other higher animals. When an infant touches an object, it then mouths it. Right from the start, reality is constantly tested on the lips.

"The mouth is serious business," says John X. "The visual and the verbal dominate modern life. The mouth is about pleasure and consumption. It's the entrance for both the divine and the pleasurable. Whatever goes into the mouth, when it comes out, is transformed. The mouth symbolizes different levels of initiation, starting with breast feeding and the pacifier. Putting a tongue in someone's mouth is a way of moving towards that person's unconscious."

Desmond Morris agrees with John X that the truth behind the mouth and the kiss is sort of spooky.

"In early human societies, before commercial baby food was invented, mothers weaned their children by chewing up their food and then passing it into the infantile mouth by lip-to-lip contact—which naturally involved a considerable amount of tonguing and mutual mouth-pressure. This almost birdlike system of parental care seems strange and alien to us today, but our species probably practiced it for a million years or more, and adult erotic kissing today is almost certainly a Relic Gesture stemming from these origins. Whether it has been handed down to us from generation to generation . . . or whether we have an inborn predisposition toward it, we cannot say. But, whichever is the case, it looks rather as though, with the deep kissing and tonguing of modern lovers, we are back again at the infantile mouth-feeding stage of the far-distant past. If the young lovers exploring each other's mouths with their tongues feel the ancient comfort of parental mouth-feeding, this may help them increase their mutual trust and thereby their pair-bonding."[1]

Through all the stages of life, the mouth connects the internal world to the external, no matter how pleasant or unpleasant that might be. As we get older, the connection gets more complicated. We need to protect that connector.

And, as we grow up, the meaning of the mouth takes on a whole new set of symbols.

In *Sexy Origins and Intimate Things,* Charles Panati writes, "Our word *puss,* meaning *face,* is from the Gaelic *pus* which was slang for *mouth.* . . . It is equally clear, linguistically, that a woman's vaginal opening was long called *a mouth*—it's one of the oldest references to *vagina.* . . . And too, a woman herself was called a cat. By gossiping she was being catty—allusions perhaps to cats' hissing, purring. . . . During the Middle Ages, both puss and pussy became female endearments."

In *The Woman's Dictionary of Sacred Symbols and Objects,* Barbara Walker explains, "Patriarchal Moslems insisted that women's mouths be covered by veils, because of the archetypal fear that equated women's mouths with the . . . toothed vagina, and saw sexual symbolism in the mouth and vice versa. . . . Copulation has often been described as female eating. In some languages, they are the same word. . . . In some societies, women were forbidden to eat anything if they could be seen by men."

Apparently, a mouth may be a bigger deal and a bigger burden than a girl is prepared to take on, at least not without a little help.

THEORY #3: LIPSTICK AND GIRLS

"Lipstick is the first thing a young girl reaches for when she starts playacting with her mother's makeup. It's no wonder—the attraction is powerful."

— MAKEUP ARTIST BOBBI BROWN[2]

Most people remember a few items and objects that they played with in their childhood. Nine out of ten times, one of those objects is lipstick. Kids find it, play with it, make a mess with it, copy their mothers with it, fall in love with it. And they seem to know it's a toy for the mouth.

"When my daughters wear lipstick, it's awakening this fantasy," says my friend Kristin. "But if they go outside with it on, I'm embarrassed. It's too powerful. By taking them out in public with the stuff on, it's like redefining the sexual makeup of a family. To do that in public is too scary, even though I know my daughter puts it on because she wants to become me, and it's not a sexual thing. Girls are drawn to lipstick like it's a magnet. It is one of the strongest first ties to connecting with the female parent."

All the kids in my friend Kevin's kindergarten class told me how much they love it when their mothers leave a lipstick mark on their face when they say good-bye and leave them.

That lipstick print is a child's way of knowing he or she is protected, and that their mother is there with them on their forehead or cheek.

Lipstick, from the outset, is presented as something good.

Something protective.

Something with a maternal magic attached.

The fact that some girls may become addicted to the stuff in the future is another matter.

THEORY #4: THE INITIATION PRINCIPAL

It is estimated that approximately half the female teenage population won't leave the house without a covering on their lips.

Out of fifty women surveyed about when they first started wearing lipstick, 80% said they started at age twelve or thirteen.

The girl can't help it—something just naturally happens at that age, where she just has to put it on. In many primitive cultures, a girl is given a colored mark on the face as she steps over the line into puberty. So are we. We use lipstick.

"Every woman is initiated into wearing lipstick, whether she remembers it or not," says my friend Judith. "There's always someone who comes up behind you, and, like, passes the wand to you. Most girls start wearing lipstick around the time they get their period."

Many women remember their initiation—remember who it was who brought them into the society of lipstick. It was usually a friend or their mother, who took them by the hand, passed the secret object, and led them over the line, over to the other side.

"It was like you had arrived," says my friend Doris. "Once you started wearing lipstick, you were there. It was the first notch in the rites of puberty. Followed by shaving your legs, boys, and cigarettes."

My friend Catherine remembers going to the makeup counter at age fourteen, with her posse of girlfriends, trying on lipsticks, experiencing the partly exotic, partly erotic thrill of turning into a woman. She easily recalls the fragrances, the excitement of walking on that bridge from girlhood to womanhood. "I'm trying on this color and that, and wonder—is this me? And can I be this? I don't know, maybe it's like shaving for boys."

Wende Zomnir, creative director for Urban Decay Cosmetics, recalls the first time she tried lipstick on, standing on her mother's vanity, leaning in toward the mirror. She remembers the smell of the lipstick, the feel of the masklike wax, and how it tasted. "It was like this addictive thing, like a drug."

Many women obtain their first lipsticks by stealing them from the drugstore or their mother.

Some claim they got their first lipstick because their mother took them shopping for it, in the same way it was done for the first bra.

My friend Julie, who was initiated by her mother, says, "It was like, 'Okay, we're going to go to the Clinique

counter. You're a big girl now, let's go get you your stuff.'
My mother finally let me wear lipstick. I guess my mouth
had finally grown up."

THEORY #5: CLOTHING AND THE MOUTH

"Lipstick may be the clothing of your words."
— MAKEUP ARTIST DIEGO DALLA PALMA

"If I don't wear lipstick I feel like I'm not wearing un-
derwear," says my friend Jenny.

"I feel invisible if I'm not wearing lipstick," is what
Lizette says. "A cup of coffee and lipstick, and then I can
face the world."

And then there's Aunt Evy.

"I can't leave the house unless I have lipstick on. It's
been that way since 1932. I won't go out the door unless
it's on. I can barely talk if I'm not wearing my lipstick. Nor,
do I think, would I want to."

As Grandma Yetta says, "For someone like me, who
grew up in the 1920s, most of the time your husband didn't
see you without your lipstick on. You didn't go to work
without lipstick. If you want me to leave the house without lipstick on today, you're asking for an accident to happen. It's like being naked. With lipstick, you're dressed."

If lipstick is a form of clothing, what does it mean if
you take your clothes off? I mean, beyond getting out the
Noxema at the end of the day. I knew who would have the
answer to this.

"It's true. Lipstick is clothes. Lipstick is like lingerie,"
says Mick Jones, the guy who owns the pornography shop
at the corner. "When you kiss, and your lipstick comes off,
it's a form of undressing. You watch a girl put lipstick on

in public, it's the undressing you're thinking of. If some-one leaves lipstick kisses all over your body, it's like a woman is dropping clothes all over your body."

John X adds to the pornography seller Jones' theory: "Talking mouths dress according to what they are going to say. How we dress the mouth reflects what we need it for, use it for, and it lets others know to what extent it is being used as a weapon."

As my friend Annette says: "If I'm wearing red lipstick, I feel I can yell at someone. If I have to talk to someone, and need to be taken seriously, I have to wear a serious color lipstick."

Annette would have gotten along in a primitive cul-ture. There, lipcoloring and marking was used to symbol-ize skill in speaking. Today, women in business are routinely told to wear dark red lipsticks when giving a speech before a group. A mouth with pale lipstick will make the audience's eyes wander.

The color of a lipstick—or the particular clothing you choose to wear for your lips—can also indicate what you are thinking without ever having to speak. As Colin, a twenty-two-year-old guy who wears black lipstick says, "My lipstick is an expression of what I think. People see my lipstick, and I don't have to say a word. They know what my general thoughts are, what group I belong to."

THEORY #6: LIPSTICK AND THE TRIBE— JOINING A TRIBE WITH YOUR LIPSTICK

Colin obviously belongs to a lipstick tribe. For the an-cients, washes and stripes of paint on the face would scare off enemy groups. Which is exactly what Colin sometimes boasts of. The ancients would mark their bodies with particular colors to let others know which tribe, or side, a person was on.

I think I choose my lipstick colors to let people in the outside world know which tribe I belong to. Makeup salespeople show me colors that will make me look professional, or trampy, or prim—to let other people know which side I am on, or could be on, or should be on.

And it's not just tribal. It's class. Status. And also an element in the pecking order within the society of women. "I think women wear lipstick for other women," says Bene-Fit Cosmetics' Jean Danielson. "It's a status thing. Eye makeup they'll put on for men. They do the eye deed for them. Amongst women, lipstick is a sign of aristocracy and pride. Of being pulled together. Within the society of women, they like knowing they're pulled together, that they're the ones on top."

"Besides," says my friend Beverly, "men will never understand lipstick. They all say they don't like it, but if they see a woman who's not wearing it, they make some comment about her looks. If the same woman wears lipstick, they'll say, 'Wow, she looks good today.' When they watch a woman put on lipstick, they always look like they're watching something they've never seen before. Some look mystified. Some look scared. Like you're a witch or something."

THEORY #7: WITCHCRAFT

American Heritage Dictionary: Witchcraft: 1. Black magic, sorcery. 2. A magical or irresistible influence, attraction, or charm. Witchery: Power to charm or fascinate. Witch: a bewitching young woman or girl.

"All women, whatever age, rank, profession or degree, whether virgins, maids, or widows that shall from and after such an Act impose upon, seduce, and betray into matrimony, any of His Majesty's subjects, by the scents, paints, cosmetics, washes, artificial teeth, false hair, Spanish wool, iron stays, hoops, high-heeled shoes, bolstered hips, shall incur the penalty of the law in force against witchcraft and the like . . ."

—ISSUED IN 1770 BY THE
BRITISH PARLIAMENT

"This is the story of a bewitchment. I was irrevocably bewitched by the power to create beauty."

—ESTÈE LAUDER, FROM THE OPENING
PAGES OF HER AUTOBIOGRAPHY,
Estèe: A Success Story

Something was going on with lipstick and witchcraft.

I decided to go to the source to have this one explained. For this, I needed to travel up to Salem, Massachusetts, where both old school and new age witches still wander the streets, sell their wares in gift shops, and tell their stories and wisdom for a few bucks. Surely one of them would be willing to explain lipstick.

As far as witches go, Lucy is pretty glamorous. At least, I think she's glamorous for a witch. I don't have a whole lot to compare her to.

What follows is Lipstick Theory According to Lucy the Witch:

"A lot of what you see in the lingo for new cosmetics is really recycled witch jargon. This popular new cosmetic word, 'infusion,' well that always meant potion. Herbs and candles, that's used to cast spells. Witches put a lot of their potions in bottles or jars, stuff with herbs and what-not that is supposed to protect you from others or from the elements. Witches use the magic of the earth to change things, so if you see anything like this in ads these days, they stole it from us.

"Painted, colored potions have long been put on the lips as a way to keep out evil spirits.

"As far as ingredients in lipstick goes, every time a fabulous new oil or herb or something is presented, it's usually something that's been used in passion spells for ages. If you see lavender in anything, remember, lavender water was worn by prostitutes to advertise who they were, and in some cases, if they were prostitutes with witchcraft abilities. What about all these cherry-flavored and scented lipsticks, especially the ones worn by teenagers? Cherries were used by witches as a love potion. By the way, roses work best in spells if the roses you use are stolen.

"And all this business about red. Purely taken from witches. It's the witch's most powerful color. Red-headed witches are more powerful, everyone knows that. And everyone knows that when a witch applies red to the face or lips it makes her more powerful. Basically, the words of the spell take on more power when the lips are red."

THEORY #8: THE ADDICTION THEORY or IS LIPSTICK A DRUG?

"If women didn't make up, they'd drink."
— REVLON'S BILL MANDEL[3]

Is lipstick a drug? I say yes. But according to the U.S. government, the answer is no. Even if the U.S. government's words hold more weight that mine, I still say yes, lipstick's a drug, and there are others who agree with me.

"Putting on lipstick is a rush, a quick fix. It's like having an espresso that recharges you," says the waitress at my neighborhood coffee shop, who always wears vibrant purple and pink lipstick.

My friend Annette has a lipstick in her pocket at all times. "When I'm nervous talking to someone," she says, "I'll slip my hand in my pocket and hold on to it. When I'm feeling a little low, I take it out and put it on. It's the most personal thing I own. It has my lip-prints all over it, it has my saliva on it, it has my breath on it. And whenever I rub it on my lips, I feel better. I feel like I'm communing with myself."

According to Grandma Ida, during the war years lipstick was all you could afford to cheer yourself up. "I think that's when the habit of buying a tube to give yourself a lift kicked in," says Ida. "It was cheap enough for the working girl to afford. After a long, tiring day, you went to the drugstore, got a vial, and it perked you up."

More and more, pharmaceutical items and vitamins are put into lipsticks.

Since the nineteenth century had its nervous breakdown, it's been the norm for makeup companies to gently fool the public into seeing cosmetics as scientific/medicinal potions which are doing community service as beautifiers.

Makeup companies choose names that hint that makeup, if used well, can be a drug. I think that is nicely expressed in the name "Prescriptives," chosen for one makeup company. And what about those clinical lab coats that the Clinique ladies wear?

"Makeup is medicine," says Lorac Cosmetics founder Carol Shaw. This from a woman whose career has been based on making over faces, and watching the person suddenly come alive with more confidence and life once the paint was on. Stila Cosmetic's Jeanine Lobell adds that a woman "comes away from a makeover feeling completely different. Suddenly, her shoulders are straight. Her chin's up."

To me, that sounds better than penicillin.

"When I put on lipstick, I feel alive," says my friend Doris.

"If I don't wear lipstick, I look sick," says Ida.

"Lipstick is necessary for the physical and emotional well being of all women," says Betty.

My friend Laura says she wears red matte lipstick to interviews, because it makes her feel more in control, and calmer.

So, lipstick can be Valium. It can be an antibiotic. It can be Ben-Gay. It can be Geritol. It can be Flintstone Multi-vitamins. Or aspirin. Or the Vitameatavegamin stuff from that episode of *I Love Lucy.*

But, like all drugs, it can be addictive.

"Once you start with the stuff, you just can't stop," says Aunt Harriett. "Once you've tasted a lipstick, that's it. You're hooked. There's no going back."

I think the best theoretical installment, however, in the "Is Lipstick a Drug? Theory" comes from the Russian Newspaper *Izvestia,* in the March 7, 1998 issue:

"A lip pomade has been discovered as a cure against Herpes of the mouth, and puts it in remission. This lipstick claims you need not get an antibiotic for Herpes as *it* acts the medicine. The ads state it annihilates the virus."

According to my neighbor Joe the medical student, it is not possible for certain drugs to be absorbed in the body through the skin. So, he says, it must be a hoax. But this is a guy who doesn't wear lipstick.

And we eat 50 percent of our lipstick.

Perhaps in the future, the medicinal power of lipstick will be used to its full advantage by creating real live medicines via a vial of Shocking Pink or Downtown Mauve.

Until that day comes, I still say, yes, lipstick is a drug.

Be it a sedative or an amphetamine, an antidepressant or a drug against madness, the answer is definitely yes.

THEORY #9: LIPSTICK AND MADNESS

It has been estimated that teenage boys consume more lipstick than anyone else, due to the longer hours of making out they tend to clock in. Perhaps lipstick is the key to understanding the social and psychological behavior of the adolescent male.

Taking on another medical job, lipstick has long played a part as an indicator of madness. When a woman draws outside the lines of the mouth, it's a sure sign of madness. My friend Rich says that a woman's lipstick color is an indicator if she's sane or wacky. "If she has on a kind of off-orangey color, and it's gone beyond the outline a little too severely, that's all I need to see to know that hey, I'm sure you mean well, but I think you've got some problems." A second indicator of madness via the lipstick thermometer is putting on a terrible color, then throwing back your head and laughing.

But beyond these extremities, lipstick itself is a slightly mad practice. "It's an OCD thing, an obsessive-compulsive thing essentially," says BeneFit Cosmetic cofounder Jean Danielson.

My friend Karen mentions having an almost hysterical need to constantly reapply her lips. "It's this sort of mad oral fixation. I think lipstick is the wand that all slightly neurotic and orally obsessed people carry."

"Lipstick plays into our confusion of identity," says John X. "Makeup ads are always asking who the real you is, and how you should let the real you shine through. Put on a lipstick and let the person inside come out. But, who's inside? And why don't I know who they are?"

THEORY #10: LIPSTICK AND FAIRY TALES

"You can put lipstick on a hog, and it's still a pig."
— POLITICIAN ANN RICHARDS, 1992[4]

"I remember when my son was a little kid, and he was in the bathroom with me. I was putting on my lipstick. He said, Mommy, what are you doing? And I said, I'm putting on my lipstick. Why? he asks. Because it makes me beautiful. He stared up at me, watching. A moment passed. And then he said, Mommy, it's not working."

— CONFESSED BY AUNT MARY
OF SAUGUS, MASSACHUSETTS

"We're all so intimate with our mouth," says BeneFit's Jean Danielson. "What's with needing a mirror to put lipstick on? Maybe they think they're turning into another person."

Maybe they are. Fairy tales and stories from antiquity onward are about magic and transformation. The Bible, medieval legends, Perrault's fairy tales—everyone gets a swing at it.

Lipstick is an essential part of your very own at-home Cinderella kit.

L'Oreal has a lipstick and makeup line called "Metamorphosis."

"The first time I had red lipstick on, I felt I was a completely different person," says my friend Beverly. "Going out with a bright red gloss is like taking on a new persona."

For Elizabeth Arden (real name: Florence Nightingale Graham), the beauty business was a fairy tale in itself. She even had it run by an imaginary character named Elizabeth Arden. She used the image of the deep red painted door—like the millionaires' homes on Fifth Avenue—as the entrance to her very own fantasy house. The whole image of the company was created around the fantasy she wanted for herself when she was younger and poor—a well-heeled, moneyed life. Through cosmetics, she was able to pretend. Through cosmetics, she was able to make it happen.

As Estée Lauder wrote in her autobiography (*Estée: A Success Story*): "In the jars and containers and tubes I sell are tiny slices of beauty—dreams come true!"

Disney's Snow White Lipstick and Nailpolish package reads: "Your smiling lips and your shining nails will help win you the prince of your dreams. Ruby Red Lip Gloss: Whether you're singing or smiling, you can pamper your lips with a gentle moisturizing lip balm. Choose from Candy Apple, Red Grape, or Wild Berry and you'll have lips no prince could resist."

Most of our earliest lipstick images come through fairy-tale characters, including Cinderella and Sleeping Beauty, who were as famous for their makeovers as anything else.

"I love lipstick," says five-year-old Sabrina. "I love dress up and pretend. When I put on lipstick, I am as pretty as Cinderella."

And once Sabrina feels she is Cinderella, she probably feels more confident in taking on the world.

THEORY #11: THE WAR PAINT THEORY— ARMOUR, CAMOUFLAGE AND DISGUISE

Once I saw a movie star in the neighborhood drugstore. There she was, venturing out into civilian territory.

She was wearing sunglasses and dark lipstick. And because of this camouflage, she was able to move about in disguise beyond the walls of stardom's castle.

Once again going back to our ancient ancestors—for them, face paint was primarily used for reasons of camouflage and warfare. Putting on colors was a way to control fear of the physical or spiritual world. I know this is what's on my mind when I'm shopping at the new age shop for a lipstick with "energy."

Tribes painted their faces into a camouflage when hunting, as a way to look fierce and brave in war, to honor the dead, and as protection against harsh wind and sun. Count me in, too, on this being why I use lipstick.

When used as disguise, it was often to trick the demons, to protect against those demons. My own urban cave is filled with tubes of red paint—this, too, evidence of a lone cavedweller's attempt to stockpile and paint on lines of red to ward off demons, wind, and other elements of the mysterious world, whatever monsters they may be.

THEORY #12: LIPSTICK AND THE VAMPIRE

Once, at a bookstore, I saw Colin, the guy who wears black lipstick, reading a book on vampires. And then it hit me: Vampires usually have the best lipstick. And lipstick ads always return every few seasons to resurrect their hero from its casket; to parade Dracula around the pages of the magazines with those blood-colored lips. The doctors in *Frankenstein* are the lab scientists trying to find ways to make and weld new skin and new cells. In *Dracula,* the doctors are Sigmund Freud clones—shrinks trying to psychoanalyze everyone, and more interested in sex, too. It was then that I decided to visit the neighborhood comic-book store about the vampiric aspect of lipstick.

What follows are the vampire lipstick theories of Joe N., comic-book store clerk.

"Vampires crave blood in order to stay alive. That's why they always look like they're wearing lipstick. It keeps them alive, that red stuff. It's true, skincare is about re-doing yourself from the outside. Making it's so you can live forever. Like Frankenstein. But Dracula is about lipstick. With the vampire's kiss you take control over someone else. The vampire's kiss means control over another, casting a spell over another. The vampire mouth gives you control, allows you to suck in outside things you want inside. When someone has plastic surgery on their lips, I think that's the closest you can get to Frankenstein and Dracula getting married."

I couldn't believe it. I was right about what I always thought about Helena Rubinstein, the great skin care specialist. She really was like Frankenstein in a couture suit.

THEORY #13: LIPSTICK AND THE DEVIL

"It must be granted that the dyeing and coloring of faces with artificial colors, and unnatural ointments is most offensive to God and derogatory to his Majesty. . . . And what are they [makeup colors] else than the Devil's intentions, to entangle poor fools in the nets of perdition."

— PHILIP STUBBES, PURITAN, 1583

Translated: Rouge your lips and go to hell.

Could this be true?

In the 1500s, pictures of devils putting lipstick on women were all too popular. In the 1300s, religious writers referred to makeup as the Devil's Soap, and mirrors as the Devil's Hiding Place. The terms Devil's Tricks and Devil's Paint have long been used to describe a woman in makeup.

And we're not just talking Middle Ages here. The term's been used well into the twentieth century.

Lipstick wearers, however, kind of like this connection.

Popular lipstick ads allude to bad girls and sin. In the typical Frankenstein vs. Dracula showdown, ads for skincare make references to a bright, new, cleaner, healthier look. Dracula and lipstick have more fun. Colors are referred to as deadly, naughty, bold, and seductive beyond seduction. The names go places eyeshadow wouldn't dare. Emotions and temperatures and taboos all get to advertise lipsticks.

Revlon's "Fire and Ice" would never have worked as a skin cream. But on the lips, there's the association with the temperatures of passion, playing with fire, and the ice maiden's freezing abilities. They're all very much at home in advertising the mouth. Sometimes, the more evil-sounding the name, the higher the sales go.

But this leads to the big question: Is lipstick evil?

Now I needed to know what God had to say about lipstick.

THEORY #14: LIPSTICK AND GOD

"God hath given you one face and you make yourself another."

— SHAKESPEARE, *Hamlet*

"In our church, wearing makeup was strictly a sin. If you wore makeup you would go straight to hell, where you would burn forever and ever. . . . Ada had put makeup on me, and God had not struck me dead. I did not feel sinful, I only felt better about myself. Then Ada pulled out of her purse the biggest sin of all—lipstick! Beautiful red lipstick! Once again she told me to hold still, and she brushed that creamy, brilliant red across my lips. We hugged and laughed and screamed and jumped up and down, two typical teenagers discovering what life was about."

— TAMMY FAYE [BAKKER] MESSNER
FROM *Tammy: Telling It My Way*

Tammy shouldn't have worried. The gods like makeup. At least the ones in ancient history did. They demanded it, actually. Painting the body and drawing on a great kisser made you more attractive to the guys upstairs. And if you wore perfume, or burned some incense, even better. This was the ultimate in religious politeness, for the gods knew you were trying hard not to offend them. And that was enough to keep anyone out of hell.

Later on, the godly rule of "Do Not Offend" moved to earth: Do not offend the person sitting next to you in the subway or sitting across from you at an interview desk. Look good. Smell good. Give yourself that finished look. And everything will be okay.

Actually, I'm not so sure the tradition of looking good for God is gone. Women still make their faces look their best for church. And when we die, most of us meet our maker in lipstick and makeup.

So why does the lipstick devil continue to stalk the planet, whispering troubling words about the evil of lipstick? Will God really be pissed off at you if you wear lipstick and try to do a better job of lips than he did?

But according to one lipstick egghead, God expects you to show up in lipstick when you die. And with nice hair. Lipstick Theory According to Wanda, the Neighborhood Hairdresser:

"The women who I work on, the older women, are about three inches from dying, yet they're all completely made up all the time. Thick, thick, heavy lipstick. Do you know what that's supposed to mean? I've thought about it for twenty years. And now I have the answer. It means you better have your lipstick on when you meet God."

But even with Wanda's sage words, I still wasn't sure—is lipstick good or evil? Is it allowed and worn in heaven? Is there a dress code in heaven, and can you take it with you?

I asked the neighborhood nun, Sister Alice, if this would all be explained someday, maybe by, like, angels or something, but Sister Alice (who, by the way, was wearing coral lipstick—allowed for nuns since Vatican II), only responded by asking me if I had thought of seeking professional counseling.

Maybe a hint of the answer comes from Estèe Lauder:

"If there is some heaven beyond earth, I'm sure it will be in the form of little angel girls on high, who could use just the teeniest dab of blusher, just the littlest drop of Super-Rich all-Purpose Creme, to make them look truly angelic. I'll be there, don't worry, to do the dabbing!"[5]

Just this one little line from Estèe gives me hope.

CHAPTER THREE

LIPSTICK FREUD

What Your Lipstick Says About You

I always thought the shape of my friend Brenda's lipstick was far more interesting than what the September issue of her favorite fashion magazine said she should wear, according to what her coloring was. Brenda's lipstick looked like a reclining chair. You could probably sit a small doll on it. And the darker the lipstick in her collection, the higher the "back" of that chair would be. The longer she used it, the sharper the point at the top would be. Once, during a very depressed period of her life, the chair became much more blunt, with a shorter back.

The magazine claimed to know Brenda and what was

right for her—but Brenda seemed to have some secrets of her own right there in her lipstick.

I immediately took her to a psychiatrist, and on the doctor's advice, the following is my own foray into a psychiatric science experiment. All data is based on real scientific investigation. All facts presented are true. Some names have been changed to protect the innocent.

Talking about and showing lipstick is one form of female bonding. Tell another woman you like her lipstick and ask what it is, and you'll be surprised at where this can lead you. She'll take it out, maybe color it on her hand, tell you why she likes it. And while she has it out, get a load of the shape of her lipstick. I never made much of this until I noticed that the only other person in the world who has the very strange, specific shape of lipstick I have is my sister Suzy. And then, of course, there was Brenda's reclining chair.

THE LIPSTICK FREUD THEORY:

I initially thought that the shape of a woman's lipstick had something to do with who she was in an obvious way—for example, if she was blunt and sharp and sleek—well, that would be her lipstick shape. If she was dull and flat and lacked shape—ditto.

But no. After spending many hours (maybe too many hours) asking women I know (and women I don't) to show me their lipstick, and after spending many hours (maybe too many hours) in my home lipstick lab, I have deduced the following:

L I P S T I C K

First of all, there are *the Basic Shapes:*

1. THE GUMBY

Inessa is a Gumby. That pointy head thing expresses Inessa's ambition. It's a movement toward a goal. The sharper the Gumby head, the stronger the drive. But Inessa has a nice roundness at the tip, which signifies the level of contentment within a Gumby. A very sharp tip spells trouble. But then, if it's too sharp, they're a Hard-Edged Nancy. The Gumby is fun-loving with a good sense of humor. Often Gumbys are embarrassed to be Gumbys. Gumbys often have a sensitive, serious side that needs to be respected. Gumbys are usually the most helpful in a crowd. They like to please others. Gumbys are good at fixing things. They make great caterers.

2. HARD-EDGED NANCY

Olivia and Joyce are Hard-Edged Nancys. That sharp edge expresses, along with a nagging perfectionism, a need for order—sometimes, but not always, a compulsive one. The Hard-Edged Nancy is honest; but also complicated. The shiny surface shows balance and insight. Hard-Edged Nancys are sometimes at odds with their love lives. Hard-Edged Nancys make great lovers. But Hard-Edged Nancys are often misunderstood. Many are prone to depression. With the right love and attention, a Nancy always shines. Nancys are good for advice and for keeping secrets. Hard-Edged Nancys are great shoppers. Often, a Hard-Edged Nancy can tell some pretty good dirty jokes.

3. THE FLATTY

My friend Susan is the typical Flatty. Level-headed and practical, a little shy, which can be taken for aloofness. She has hidden artistic flair. When the chips are down, and you find out who your friends really are, don't be surprised if you find the Flatty running to your rescue. Flatties can be insecure worriers. But Flatties almost always are good for saying what you need to hear, and saying it well. Flatties are often neat. Flatties have good memories. Flatties usually have a fabulous romantic streak. Flatties know how to get the job done. Flatties should show their lipsticks at job interviews.

4. THE RECLINING CHAIR

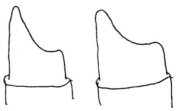

Ruth, Sarah, and Brenda are all Reclining Chairs of different sorts. What most signifies a Reclining Chair is their friendliness. Chairs love their friends and making new friends. Reclining Chairs like activity, and are usually the first to turn a dull scene into a party. Reclining Chairs are unique in personality. Reclining Chairs are the type most prone to metamorphose into something else. Reclining Chairs change often. Pay attention to your Reclining Chair friends when this happens. Reclining Chairs often will have higher backs on their work lipsticks, and shorter backs on their going-out lipsticks. High backs on Reclining Chairs usually signify stress. A word to Reclining Chairs: For optimum health, always monitor the back of your chair.

5. THE BULLET (ROUND BETTY)

Betty was a Bullet. So was Beatrice. When I found out Belinda was also a Bullet, I realized the true Round Betty persona. They tend to be quieter and softer. Often, a Bullet is not what she appears to be. There's an intensity in a Bullet, and it takes time to really find the person within—but when you do, she is always loving, smart, and full of surprises. Bullets are known for their intelligence. Bullets often have a good sense of direction, and good taste. Bullets can be trouble when they get mad. Bullets can hold a grudge and be very talented at revenge. Often, later in life, Bullets undergo big changes and rediscoveries. During this time, they will most often become Daggers or Reclining Chairs. Be good to a Bullet; they usually can help you out down the road, especially in business.

6. THE PACIFIER (OR, THE EMPIRE STATE BUILDING)

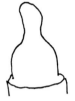

My sister Suzy is a Pacifier. So is her daughter Alina, who has taken to wearing lipstick at age four (it runs in the family). I am a Pacifier. I haven't yet met many Pacifiers. However, I have been told there are a lot of Pacifiers in Germany. A curved, amorphous or strange shape signifies a need to buy more clothing. Anything resembling a pacifier top is a dead giveaway for a love of chocolate. An Empire tip shows the need to change apartments. A strong Empire base signifies the need to be paid back the money that one of your friends hasn't paid since 1984.

7. THE DOUBLE-EDGED SWORD

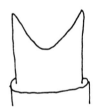

I work with someone who is a DES—or Double-Edged Sword. Her name will be changed to protect her innocence—let's call her Darlene. If a sharp point means you have a specific goal, two signifies being torn in two directions, conflicting interests, or many talents. Darlene and other DESs finds warmth in a steady group of friends. They like to nurture those who are hurting, and place importance on family. DESs are fashion conscious, and loyal. But beware—cross a DES, and you're screwed.

8. THE DAGGER AND
THE LEANING TOWER OF PISA

Rhonda, who I've known since seventh grade, is a Dagger. Forthright, strong, opinionated. Daggers are impulsive. Daggers tend to show up in places you wouldn't expect. Daggers have a great curiosity and love to travel. Daggers can be dangerous if you let them. Beware of a Dagger's temper. But like all sharp objects, Daggers are exciting. Daggers also exist in a Leaning-Tower-of-Pisa variety, like Megg. Leaning Towers of Pisa love to talk. They're usually the first to hear new gossip. Leaning Towers of Pisa should not show their lipsticks to potential landlords. Leaning Towers like to party. When a Leaning Tower has a crisis, the tower often falls, and it is best for her to comfort herself with a gallon of ice cream.

The Leaning Tower of Pisa that appears suddenly is often a sign of instability.

10. THE TEARDROP

Greta is a pure Teardrop. Greta is responsible for initiating a whole new area of study in Lipstick Freud. When I looked at Greta's lipstick, I saw a teardrop whittled into the end. Greta, who never cried. This was her inner need speaking out. Her lipstick shape was her way of whittling out her inner need. I've witnessed variations on the Teardrop. I've seen the Heart at the end of Laura's lipstick—the always lovelorn Laura. And the letter S at the end of Barbara's lipstick (I haven't figured that one out yet). Teardrops and their cousins show us the wearer's inner secrets, truths, and desires—whittled by mouths into a piece of wax. If you are a Teardrop, don't show your lipstick to anyone.

LIPSTICK FREUD SUBCATEGORIES:

The house: In six separate case studies, women whose lipstick started resembling a house were also found to be moving toward more domestic inclinations in their lives. It also indicates a move toward balance in general.

The hat: In two studies, the hat has been found to be symbolic of a person who is trying to get away from something, or who is actively planning on or secretly thinking of leaving soon.

The swirl: The indicator of kindness. If you seen this at the end of someone's lipstick, you know they're a good egg.

A word of warning to all: Be careful and beware. If you are a woman who wants to protect and preserve her mystery, keep your lipstick in your bag. You never know who could be asking to see it. It could be a trick. You never know who can cull knowledge about your inner being, and who they might tell.

And then, of course, don't think the shape alone will give away all your inner secrets. Because, of course, there's the Lipstick Freud of—

HOW YOU PUT YOUR LIPSTICK ON AND WHAT THAT SAYS ABOUT YOU:

At some points in the twentieth century, putting on lipstick was considered a hideous act—a very private act, which should be confined to the bathroom.

From Mrs. Oliver Harriman's *Beauty Etiquette Book,* 1942: "Applying lipstick in public is supposed to outrage good taste at all times. I would rather see a girl . . . putting lipstick on her lips than going wan-lipped, but she who does this in the presence of a man just isn't using good sense. The very purpose of makeup is to create the illusion of beauty. Girls, the next time you put on lip makeup in front of your mirror, just look at the gyrations you perform with your mouth. Since this ritual isn't an attractive sight, don't let men observe it too closely."

Since then, not everyone has listened to Mrs. Harriman.

According to Dr. Robertson, neighborhood psychiatrist, the way you put on your lipstick says something about the way you communicate with the world orally. It gently communicates how you feel about your lips.

According to the neighborhood veterinarian, it doesn't mean anything. But what does he know?

The Major Categories are:

1. The Joker's Smile Method: You want to get the most out of life that you can. This person loves to make big statements, and is often a big exaggerator.

2. The Jutting Upper Lip Method: A need to question and scrutinize is characteristic. Also, this is usually a religious or moral person.

3. The Puckering Penelope Method: A systematic, intense, and rigorous person, who pays attention to details.

4. Careful Slow Methodical Method: The name says it all.

5.   The Sucking Method: The ultimate in the orally fixated.

6.   The Terrified Face Method: Indicates a person who is still a little afraid of putting on lipstick.

LIPSTICK FREUD ADDENDUM:

According to makeup artist Bobbi Brown, in her book *Bobbi Brown Beauty,* if your lipstick is flat (i.e., a Flatty) you're probably applying to bottom lip only and then smacking them together . . . and maybe missing coverage in corners. If you have what Brown refers to as a pyramid shape (for our purposes, a House) you're probably doing it evenly on both sides, and getting the corners. If you have a long point on one side (which, in my lingo, could be a Gumby or a Chair), you're probably putting lips together around the tube, and maybe getting too much in the corners of your mouth.[1]

FREUDIAN PURSEOLOGY:

But just when you thought you were safe if you just kept your lipsticks in your purse and didn't let anyone see, the Handbag Freuds come and get you. Now even your purse gives you away. Here's one more thing to feed your paranoia, from *The Language of Clothes,* by Alison Lurie (now you'll never leave the house):

"The term 'purse' for the female pudenda dates from the early seventeenth century. The common phrase 'old bag' for an unattractive, aging woman is about a hundred years old, and may be subliminally responsible for the female readiness to discard even a slightly worn purse. . . . Its content . . . may represent the contents of the mind, or serve as both a portable identity kit and a repair kit. . . . According to male informants, a tightly snapped, zipped, and buckled purse suggests a woman who guards her physical and emotional privacy closely, one whom it will be difficult to get to know in either the common or biblical sense. On the other hand, a tote with an open top, Lurie writes, is the bag of a lady who's more emotionally open—and sexually accessible as well.

Wait. This is only the tip of the iceberg in Lipstick Freud.

On a recent trip to Northern California, I came across a woman named Sun Ray Winter, who reads lipstick prints.

For real. For a living. In the same way a palm would be read. "Lipstick Print Reading" is what she calls it. That's what it says on her card. And as soon as she gets a shingle, it will say that too.

Sun Ray's practice involves one part "mouth reading," or Asian healing (as she explains it) and one part Bull (as some of her neighbors explain it).

The Asian healing principals she uses to read the mouth go something like this:

If you have a small mouth, you're one of those yin types. If you have a large mouth, you're one of those yang types.

If you have a horizontal line right above your nose, you're having sex problems.

If your upper lip is a little too big, you're prone to enjoying life too much—a real partier.

If you're one of those yin types, you're a stomach-based personality.

If you have a big lower lip, you may be prone to secrecy.

The upper lip reveals your passion for food and love. Too many lines on the top lip means you're getting too much action in that area.

A lot of lines on the bottom lip means you are working too hard; carefully spaced lines means you will be doing well soon in business.

Your lifeline is the center line of your bottom lip.

I think Sun Ray is pushing it a little. Possibly jealous of an eye-makeup obsessed friend who was bragging that eyes have their own practitioners (iridologists), and aware that hand and foot fetishists have their own readers, she was hell-bent on creating a branch of medicine for the lipstick obsessed.

Sun Ray will also let you know how you're doing in terms of money, love life, or career. Forget about what the fortune cookie has to say about your future.

Lip-print reading is still under further investigation by myself, and perhaps soon, by the Federal Government and the American Association of Astrologers and Psychics as well.

Who knows, maybe it is the tarot of the future. Or maybe not.

CHAPTER FOUR

LIPSTICK FACT AND FICTION

POLITICALLY INCORRECT LIPSTICK: The Roman Emperor Elagabalus, who came to power in 218 A.D. at age fifteen through the manipulations of a creepy-crawly mother and grandmother, was known to stroll through the streets surrounded by naked eunuchs and behaving so perversely that even the famously decadent Romans thought he was pushing it. He wore garish silks and tacky jewels, and his lips were painted up in a shocking blue. Perhaps it was this very bad choice of lipcolor that the Romans considered to be the last straw—he didn't stay emperor for long.

HEY CHARLES, HELENA, AND LIZ: EAT YOUR HEART OUT: In the Islamic world of 840 A.D., Blackbird, a famous singer from Baghdad, opened the first known full-fledged beauty institute in southern Spain, where he taught comprehensive makeup application to his disciples, including the fine art of lipcoloring.

SECRET AMERICAN HISTORY: Historians have uncovered documents detailing the daily practices of George Washington. He was a womanizing, vain sort of fellow, and along with his Caswell-Massey perfumes, dentures, and powdered wigs, some scribes believe that our father George may also have taken to periodically wearing lipstick.

LIPSTICK WILL KILL YOU . . . Literally. During the French Revolution, the wearing of lipstick or any kind of makeup was a sign that you sympathized with the aristocracy, and anyone seen wearing it was condemned to the guillotine. Marie Antoinette can be blamed for the disappearance of the Golden Age of Men in Lipstick, as it was during this time that all guys quickly smeared the stuff away in order to save their lives.

GIVE ME LIPSTICK OR GIVE ME DEATH: Madame Pompadour, known for her laborious makeup rituals, sat up in her deathbed and summoned her exhausted servant with her famous last words: "Bring me my pots of rouge." She put the stuff on, then dropped dead.

LIPSTICK WILL SAVE YOUR LIFE: The publication *Emergency Medicine* documents the following case: A woman suffered a head-on auto collision while wearing her seat belt. There were few external signs of possible internal damage—but there was a lipstick print on the left breast area of her clothes. Under normal conditions, kissing your own breast is no easy feat. The lipstick trace thus led the doctors to their finding: A separation of the vertebral column allowed the neck to move that far. And from there, she was fixed up and saved. Thanks, lipstick.

LIPSTICK TATTOOS AND OTHER ACCIDENTS: George Burchett, famed for his coronation tattoos of 1910, was the most famous tattoo artist in Britain for years. His business also involved work as a "Beauty Doctor." If a woman wanted a rosy glow, George injected dyes into the lips and cheeks, sometimes with such terrible results that women had permanent "full-face tattoos" of bizarrely hued reds and browns.

CZAR NICHOLAS AND ALEXANDRA MAY HAVE MORE TO DO WITH YOUR LIPSTICK THAN YOU THINK: While we generally associate Coco Chanel's contributions to fashion, perfume, and red lipstick to her very French aesthetic, in actuality her work was more than slightly influenced by the Russians. After the fall of the last czar, her headquarters were heavily staffed with deposed Russian aristocrats—working as office help, body mannequins, face models, and styling assistants. Perhaps when we think of that perfect red lipstick as the ultimate French color, we're really seeing the glow of borscht.

REASON FOR UNEMPLOYMENT: BAD LIPSTICK: The right lipstick and makeup could make or break a screen actress' career in the silent film era. Film, lighting, and makeup hadn't quite figured one another out yet, and the wrong colors had monstrous results on screen. Actresses lined up at the door of makeup artist Max Factor at dawn, waiting to have their faces done for screen tests. Knowing a good thing when he had it, Max quickly became a lipstick obsessive-compulsive, opened a laboratory in Hollywood, and invented the Kissing Machine. A male and female dummy head came together and apart at the flip of a switch, in Max's quest for the ultimate movie-perfect kissproof lipstick. Max also built a Blonde, Brunette, and Redhead Room at his lab, where only lipsticks particular to each room's color were allowed, and he set to work on the study of perfect color coordination.

ONE OF THE FIRST KNOWN REFERENCES TO THE "GENERATION GAP" came in 1925, when people referred to the gap between generations of mother and daughter being signified by one wearing lipstick and the other not.

LIPSTICK TO CALM THE NERVES: In 1928, a beauty parlor, complete with a full line of lipsticks, was put into effect as a key part of the treatment for patients at a New Jersey insane asylum. The practice continues today, at various institutions worldwide, with many accounts of therapeutic success.

LIPSTICK NEARLY RUINS COLETTE: French writer Colette, best known for *Gigi,* opened a salon in Paris in the 1930s, saying "the transformation of women's faces was certainly very amusing." Unfortunately, the business folded, but thank God she didn't give up her day job, which she had to go back to: writing. Later, Audrey Hepburn, whom Colette discovered as the one to play

Gigi on the stage, would become the muse for Givenchy's clothes, perfumes, and lipstick—personifying the ideal look for lips in the fifties.

AFTER TWO BIZARRE DEATHS BY EYELINER IN 1938, the Food and Drug Administration finally decided to include makeup as a product it must monitor. A few more eye-paint deaths occurred, as did a substantial number of peroxide-related ones (for Jean Harlow wannabes). Lipstick unfortunately also joined the roster of Makeup's Grim Reaper, but since the lipstick incidents continue to be played down in the annals of eerie makeup history, and the others dually played up, many writers on fashion and cosmetics have been led to proclaim that lipstick is the safest cosmetic.

MR. ROOSEVELT, HOW CAN I HELP THE WAR EFFORT? In her autobiography, Helena Rubinstein wrote of asking the president what she could do to aid the battle. Mr. R answered with the story of a woman in London being carried on a stretcher during the Great Blitz. Before she agreed to take a sedative, she insisted she put her lipstick on, explaining that the lipstick "just does something for me." And with the story told, Mr. Roosevelt let Helena know her patriotic duties as a Good American had already been done.

MARY QUANT was a great innovator in lipstick, creating the famous flower vial and revolutionary colors, but she caused problems in her other pursuits. Quant also invented the miniskirt, and protests arose outside the Vatican when women wearing her creation were barred from entering. Wearers were also subject to jail in Greece—and perhaps the most horrible of all—were banned in

America from entering Disneyland. These women should have just stuck to the Quant lipsticks, which came without such heavy restrictions.

FEAR AND LOATHING AT HARPER'S BAZAAR . . . Filmmaker Stanley Kubrick looked through fashion mags to find ideas for his movie characters, and after studying the editorials and ads for eye makeup and lipstick, came up with the face for the creepily done-up Malcolm McDowell in *A Clockwork Orange*.

QUESTIONS: WHERE DID FREE GIFT WITH PURCHASE COME FROM? Answer: Estèe Lauder. She started the practice of giving out free samples, as a gift, to encourage word of mouth. Her competitors thought this was the sure sign of a nut—and the sure sign of a quick fold to her company. They watched from the sidelines as she "gave away the store," taking bets on how long it would take for her to go out of business. The laughter soon turned to imitation, and then, in no time, standard house practice.

HOW MANY PEOPLE DOES IT TAKE TO SCREW IN A LIPSTICK? Well, if you're Doris Day, twenty-two. Word has it she had this number of makeup men to do her face.

KNOW YOUR INSULTS: If you are going to insult someone about their lipstick color, and tell them they look like a hooker, be sure you have your insult factoids correct. If she's on her way to talk with a man in the military, it may be a compliment. The word *hooker* originated in the Civil War, where a General Hooker made a practice of bringing in girls to boost the morale of his soldiers—otherwise known as "Hooker's Girls."

LIZ AND HER LIPS: In *Liz: An Intimate Biography of Elizabeth Taylor,* Liz mythologizer C. David Heymann tells how lipstick got bigger billing in the life of Liz than the average Joe. On the set of *Between Friends* all extras were instructed to wear "a neutral sort of flesh-colored lipstick," but when a makeup man applied red lipstick to one red-headed extra, an authority on the set hollered: "Get it off her, nobody but Elizabeth wears red." Heymann also recounts how, during the filming of *Cleopatra,* Liz insisted on wearing makeup for every scene, even if she was told she didn't need it. One top crew member reported walking into her dressing room, where "she had her mouth open and was even dabbing powder on the roof of her mouth. 'What are you doing?' I asked, and she replied, 'Well, they'll see inside my mouth when I speak my lines. I want to look perfect.' "

THE CASE OF THE ZOMBIE BARDOTS: According to a biography by Jeffrey Robinson, the famous Bardot lips that launched a million wanna-bes, and a million Bardot-inspired lipsticks, may have actually been the outcome of lip hypnotism. Husband Roger Vadim allegedly taught Bardot how to pout, how to use her mouth when she ate, and generally brainwashed her into her entire persona, the one with lips and the one without. So maybe the look so many have tried to copy is not Brigitte at all. Maybe, without knowing it, a million women have been trying all this time to look just like a Stepford Wife.

THE TRUTH BEHIND MARILYN'S MOUTH: Marilyn Monroe's lips were another marker on the timeline of history, and one that became a twentieth-century icon all on their own—her always slightly parted mouth. The truth behind the pout, however, was what the movie studios saw as a defect. Marilyn had a rather prominent chin, made more pronounced with a closed mouth. With open lips, suddenly, you didn't see the "fault," and a lip icon was made.

AND THE TRUTH BEHIND BARBIE: Another lipstick role model came via the Barbie doll. But the truth behind Barbie's lips is due to another defect—of character, you might say. Barbie's mouth, coveted by girls for decades, is actually modelled on Barbie's true predecessor, the 1950s German gold-digging floozy doll, Lilli. Lilli wasn't a toy for girls, but for men. Her lips were fashioned in the style of a tramp, and if a man gave Lilli as a gift to a woman, it was a way of letting her know that he expected more than just dinner—but rather something that Lilli might do, lips and all.

PERFECT TEETH FOR PERFECT LIPS: For an era that looked down on painting the mouth, nineteenth-century beauty manuals were strangely obsessed with dictating the mandates of a perfect mouth. Chapters called "Toilet for the Lips" included hints on how to control the shape of your lips through thinking appropriate thoughts, and how the smell of your breath was also controlled through thought. The most important thing, however, was the perfect set of teeth. Perfect teeth equaled the ultimate in oral chic. Another toothy fashion trend was in sixteenth- to seventeenth-century Japan. After applying white powder, rouge, and a lovely red lip paint, it was suggested a woman then blacken out her teeth to bang up the look.

CAN LIPSTICK MAKE YOU LIVE FOREVER? Vaseline has joined the pantheon of lipstick by adoption. Almost every major makeup artist will include a tip or hint that throws Vaseline somewhere into the mix. Vaseline's inventor, Robert Augustus Chesebrough, would surely be pleased to hear this if he were alive today. But Chesebrough did some unusual advertising of his own during his life. The great inventor, who lived to be ninety-six, pronounced that eating a spoonful of Vaseline daily did the longevity trick.

THIN TIGHT LIPS HOLDING LIPSTICK SECRETS: What do Biba's Barbara Hulanicki, Coco Chanel, Helena Rubinstein, and Elizabeth Arden have in common? Thin lips. But in many of their ads, a wider mouth is what is encouraged, since thin lips are often a symbol of (among other things) a person who's holding back secrets.

BRAWLERS FOR BEAUTY: While the first department store makeup counter was opened at B. Altman's in 1867 in New York, during the 1840s a full-time cosmetic artist was a standard fixture at many upscale pharmacies. But most of the time, it wasn't helping out with a lipstick choice and application that these makeup artists did, but rather covering up black eyes for men who had come in off the street after a brawl.

LIPSTICK ON MR. ED: In 1966, Elizabeth Arden's *New York Times* obituary read: "She treated women like horses and horses like women." True. Down at the stable, Liz used her famous Eight-Hour Cream and other Arden beautifying products on her prize race horses, rubbing them until they glowed. And it was no secret that the stable workers thought she was a bit of a weirdo. To this day, however, it is still to be determined whether or not she painted any of her trademark pink lipsticks onto the horses' lips. No one at the stables will talk. It is also still to be determined whether or not Liz was a fan of the television show *Mr. Ed,* and if she had any secret dreams of working as the talking horse's personal makeup artist, changing his image to one of a more glamorous, lipsticked stud. No one at the stables is talking on that one either.

THE FAILURE HALL OF FAME: Studies show that 80–90% of all new consumer products bomb big time. The roster of celebrities who came out with makeup companies (or makeup divisions) that never quite lived on include: Lillian Russell, Sarah Bernhardt, Zsa Zsa Gabor, Farrah Fawcett, Dolly Parton (sold at her amusement park, Dollywood), Calvin Klein, Ralph Lauren, Mary Pickford (six shades of lipstick at sixty cents each), and Constance Bennett. Constance, by the way, is credited with being the first celebrity to do a television makeup commercial, not for herself, but for Miss Arden. Other scenes from the Lipstick Failure Hall of Fame include Clairol Lipsticks in the 1960s, formulated to match haircolor, and Revlon's attempt at making its own version of the hypoallergenic Clinique, a short-lived production called Etherea.

IF THEY ONLY KNEW . . . THE MEDIEVAL POPES WOULD BE ROLLING OVER IN THEIR GRAVES: On signing or sealing a love letter, common practice has us smacking down a lipstick kiss print, drawing the letter *X* and *O* next to it and sometimes scribbling in SWAK (sealed with a kiss). In the early Christian era, the *X* (or cross) was the standard John Hancock of the illiterate set. If a medieval guy really wanted to prove he meant business, a kiss mark was added as a double whammy of sincerity. Somehow things change. Kisses and

X-marks look at each other differently over time. The flirtatious and erotic connotations the two now have when placed side by side are not, I don't think, what the popes had in mind.

LIPSTICK TRACES ALL OVER NEW YORK: What was one of the main inspirations for the symbolic red door of Elizabeth Arden? When little Florence Nightingale Graham, as she was then called, arrived in New York, she would walk up and down Fifth Avenue, looking at the millionaires' mansions with their fabulously large doors, painted in deep, rich colors. Soon her own door came, and she'd later describe this red as the wonderful color of lipstick.

PROZAC LIPSTICK: Elizabeth and Charles and Estèe and Helena were known to sneak around one another with such anger and paranoia in the 1950s that it seemed in time the madness would seep into the lipstick, or at least subconsciously attract a psychiatric specialist to step in. Maybe in a way it did. Eli Lily, the maker of Prozac, eventually bought Elizabeth Arden.

SILENT STAR LOUISE BROOKS did her part to popularize the painted mouth in the 1920s, but not much credit is given today to her mother, who also did her part for lipstick liberation. Myra Brooks, a feminist on the women's club lecture circuit in the twenties, stood before the crowds with her message that "women of today have a right to use every artifice, in reason and with harmony, to make themselves attractive." Myra was also a beauty scribe, writing a book called *Health, Beauty and Psychology.* Unfortunately, no copies have survived, but her beauty hints and beauty philosophy live on in the films of her daughter.

SOME STRANGE ATTEMPTS AT LIPSTICK BY MEN? In the nineteenth century, German students held duels with the sole purpose of getting face scars, including cuts on the mouth and the skin around it, which would then become status symbols. Red wine was next poured onto the fresh scar to really make it glow. Maybe someone should have told them it would have been easier to just draw on some liprouge.

THE QUEEN'S LIPSTICK: Queen Elizabeth II of England had a special lipstick concocted for her 1952 coronation to match her purple and crimson robes. The royal lipstick, a soft red-blue, even got its very own name: The Balmoral Lipstick, named after her Scottish country home.

JEZEBEL earns the prize as Most Evil Woman in the Bible. Of the many things she did wrong, she got everybody to worship Baal, killed some prophets, and, worst of all, wore far too much makeup. Jezebel is credited as the creator of darkly painted lips that symbolize the stereotypical evil woman that continued through fairy tales, comic books, Theda Bara, and television bad girls such as Joan Collins in *Dynasty*. She also was one of the early founders of makeup as disguise. Jez painted her face in order to hide from her murderer, Jehu (he eventually killed her by tossing her out of a window). As the ultimate insult to her overuse of makeup, only her hands, feet, and head were found among her remains—the parts of her body she'd covered with the most makeup. Supposedly the dogs ate her—but even they couldn't stomach such terrible makeup. Although purple has been suspected as Jez's color of choice, scholars are still debating the style and textures of the lipstick she used. Maybe it was the cheap stuff in the fifty-nine-cent bin—last season's colors gone rancid.

KISSOLOGY FACT AND FICTION: In primitive societies, the hot breath that comes out of the mouth was thought to be a person's soul, and when two people kissed, their two souls were connecting. Other kiss theorists explain the origin of the smooch as the way in which two people used to sniff each other out (just like dogs do). For ancient Romans, the final kiss given to someone on his deathbed was the way to catch the dying person's soul. In Mongolia, a man must not kiss his son on the face. He may, however, smell the boy's head. Some African tribes with stretched or heavily marked lips do not kiss. In ancient Japan and China, lip kissing was not practiced. When gauche European tourists showed up in the 1500s and took to kissing in public, the natives practically passed out at such a lurid spectacle.

KAMA SUTRA LONG-LASTING BERRY STAIN: According to the *Kama Sutra,* the perfect woman should be skilled in sixty-four arts. Number six: tattooing. Number nine: coloring the teeth, mouth, hair, nails, body, and clothes.

WITCHCRAFT, TWENTIETH-CENTURY STYLE? In the 1700s, a British woman could be arrested if it was determined that she wore lipstick, among other cosmetics, in an attempt to bewitch and trick a man into marriage. In Kansas, it was put on the books in 1915 that any woman under forty-four would be slapped with a misdemeanor if she wore lipstick, powder, and rouge for the very evil purpose of creating "a false impression."

THE SUPERMODEL CRAZE ISN'T ANYTHING NEW: While big-lipped fashion models may have taken some of the spotlight away from movie stars in dictating how women are supposed to look, before the movie stars there were the PBs (Professional Beauties). These women were quite the rage in the 1870s—mobbed in the streets, and written about in excruciating detail in magazines and newspapers. In keeping with the Victorians' obsession with lips, the PBs' mouths almost always got heavy coverage in these write-ups, reverently described as soft pink and slightly parted. As soon as an article appeared where a PB's mouth was depicted as swollen, large, or dark, it was a signal that she was on her way to being KO'd as a PB.

CHANEL NO. 5 DO YOU FEEL LUCKY?: Superstitious Coco Chanel viewed the number five as a symbol of good luck, and on the fifth day of the fifth month of 1921, she introduced her No. 5 fragrance. Eight years later, she introduced the No. 5 lipstick in the fabulously lucky year the stock market crashed. Oh well. Good luck did prevail in the end though. For almost seventy years, it has been one of the most sought after lipsticks in history.

LIPSTICK AS A FORM OF ESCAPE AND IMMIGRATION: Max Factor got his start working closely with the mouth at age eight, as a dentist's apprentice. He then went on to become the official wig maker and cosmetologist for the family of Czar Nicholas. In an act similar to one from the Hollywood melodramas he'd later do the lipstick for, when Max couldn't take his life as a royal servant any longer, he used his own makeup kit, stocked with liprouge and grease paint, as his visa for escape. Max got out his tubes and lubes and made himself look deathly sick, all pallid lips and ashen skin. He was quickly ordered to make his way to the infirmary, but instead, Max kept going, and escaped to America.

LIPSTICK BUSINESS OR MEDICAL SCHOOL?

Elizabeth Arden (Florence Nightingale Graham) was a nursing school dropout. Helena Rubinstein was a medical school dropout. Helena preached the Science of Beauty. Elizabeth chose the more nurselike rehabilitative approach, beauty enhanced through yoga and exercise. Helena spent hours in her laboratory, and instituted the practice of having a doctor in the salon at all times. Long before Jane Fonda came along, Liz made exercise class part of her salon, and made the first exercise follow-along-with-me recording.

ETYMOLOGY OF A LIPSTICK: *Lippa sticka,* Old English, dates from approximately 1000 A.D. The word *glamorous,* of Scottish origin, meant enchantment or spell (derived from *glamer,* or *grammar,* then becoming the term for public outcry, scandal, or loud noise, and soon, a magic spell that stirred one's imagination). In 1889, *lip stick* became part of everyday English usage, but only in relation to the evil stuff actors wore. In 1915, *lip stick* crawled out of theater-only lingo and became the word for the popular wax in stick form that even nice people were wearing. In the mid- to late 1920s, the two separate words *lip* and *stick* finally got pushed together and made the complete *lipstick,* all melted into one word, and was indoctrinated into standard dictionary usage.

MORE LIPSTICK ETYMOLOGY: The term *oomph* that is commonly used to describe a potent and sexy lipstick color, was first created by some Hollywood press agents in the 1940s (rumored to be an imitation of an orgasmic sigh). A second popular lipstick word, *vamp,* has its origins in the Tartar noun for witch, or casting spells. And a third word typically found in lipstickeze: *fox,* or *foxy,* has its origins in the black South (popularized when Muhammad Ali used it in a 1963 *Time* magazine interview).

HARPER'S INDEX OF LIPSTICK or LIPSTICK NUMEROLOGY—A RUNDOWN OF LIPSTICK STATISTICS:

- Number of dollars spent in 1946 on cosmetics in America: $700 million.

- Among the 50 million women who were users in the 1946 survey:
    Percentage of women who used lipstick: 99.
    Percentage who used nail polish: 95.
    Percentage who used perfume: 73.
    Percentage who used face cleanser: 71.

- Percentage of annual profit increase for the cosmetics industry since 1975: 10 (the highest amount being in the South, followed by the West, the Northeast, and the Midwest).

- Amount of dollars spent on lipstick worldwide in 1986: $580 million, with another $140 million for lip gloss.

- Number of lipsticks bought by women in the United Kingdom in 1997: 45 million.

- Number of lipsticks bought by women in Germany in 1996 (where there are 25% more women than in the UK): 3.5 million.

- Number of dollars Americans spent on cosmetics in 1996: $4.7 billion.

- Highest scorer in a survey of what men find themselves looking at in assessing a sex partner: the mouth.

- According to William Cane's *The Art of Kissing,* percentage of men who don't mind kissing a woman wearing lipstick: 67.
    - Percentage who actually like it if the lipstick is flavored: 8.
    - Percentage who don't enjoy kissing a woman in lipstick, because of its taste or smell: 25.

- Percentage of expendable income Americans shell out on cosmetics: 6–10 (double for teenagers).

- Percentage of American women who wear foundation: 50 (as opposed to the estimated 85% who will wear lipstick).

- Percentage of women in a 1998 *Jane* magazine poll who own over 20 lipsticks: 32. Percent who own less than ten: 34.

- Average size of a lipstick bullet upon purchase: one-quarter-inch.

- Average number of hours promised for one application of long-wear lipsticks: 5.

- Average number of hours promised in a long-wear lipstick: 1,325 per tube.

- Average life of a lipstick tube used regularly: six months to one year.

- According to one *Allure* magazine article, the number of lipsticks one typical American woman goes through yearly: 5.

- Percentage of American women who apply lipstick every single day: 55 (while only 16% put on liner daily).

CHAPTER FIVE

HOW TO GROW A LIPSTICK

Inside the Lipstick Chamber

Secrecy is the rule of thumb at most lipstick companies. Perhaps this has something to do with lipstick's rich history as a playground for theft, blackmail, phone tapping, and spying.

Potions and secret ingredients can be guarded as closely as the recipes for New Coke and McDonald's Secret Sauce might have been. The process by which lipstick is made, however, has not changed that much over the years. The first-known lipstick found at Ur was made of a base of white lead. That, at least, is a thing of the past.

Modern lipsticks are a fairly simple concoction: Lipstick = an oil-wax base + coloring agents + a trace amount of fragrance.

Lipsticks will then incorporate other ingredients to soften them, shine them up, matte them down, and so forth. Pigments are ground up and mixed with melted waxes and oils. The mixture is then heated, cooled, flamed, boxed, and sent on its way to the shiny glass display cases of the makeup counter nearest you.

What follows is some of what goes on in the process of making the stuff.

A Crash Course in How
Lipstick Is Made

OILS, PIGMENTS, EMOLLIENTS, AND WAX:

THE BASE is what gives lipstick its adherence, as well as its overall ability to last and hold up. Bases are made of oils, waxes, and emollients.

WAXES are the most durable and thickest of all ingredients used in lipsticks. It is the wax that really gives a lipstick its shape. Carnauba, beeswax, and castor oil are the most commonly used ingredients. A blend of the three is essential for maintaining shape and ease of application (if it was just a hard wax texture, you would basically be making a candle). Carnauba is the wax with the highest melting temperature, so this is a popular ingredient, since this means a lipstick with Carnauba wax has less of a chance of melting in your pocketbook in hot weather.

THERE IS A BALANCE BETWEEN OIL AND WAX for the type and texture of lipstick. Lip gloss has more oil, less wax. Long-lasting color-stay lipsticks use oil-like ingredients (such as voletile silicone) that evaporate quickly on the lip's surface.

OILS are usually mineral, castor, lanolin, or petrolatum.

EMOLLIENTS are soothing and protective agents which disperse pigment and give the lipstick some moisturizing properties. They give a lipstick its texture (lanolin, castor oil, esters), and carry the pigments to the lips.

COLORING AGENTS ARE PIGMENTS AND DYES:

PIGMENTS are ground into the base; rather than being absorbed into the skin, pigments stick to the skin's surface. A good lipstick will have pigments that are very finely ground and well distributed throughout the base, creating an even, smooth texture.

DYES are used in long-lasting lipsticks and are more often absorbed into the skin. Heavier dyes were found in lipsticks of the 1930s–50s. Insoluble dyes are *lakes*.

PERFUME AND FLAVORINGS are used to disguise the natural odor and taste of the waxes, emollients, oils, thickeners, and thinners.

ALMOST ALL OTHER INGREDIENTS are used to give the lipstick various sheens and consistencies.

CHEMISTS CITE SIX BASIC INGREDIENTS THAT ARE ESSENTIAL FOR MAKING A LIPSTICK:

Beeswax, carnauba wax, candelilla wax, castor oil, lanolin and ozokerite (a waxlike thickener).

A TYPICAL APPROXIMATE PERCENTAGE BREAKDOWN OF THE MAIN COMPONENTS IN A LIPSTICK:

Castor oil: 65%

Beeswax: 15%

Carnauba wax: 8–10%

Lanolin: 5%

Colorants

A trace amount of fragrance

MAKING A LIPSTICK:

Once a lipstick is formulated, it will undergo various breakage and temperature tests, to be sure it can withstand the activity inside a handbag, different geographic climates, and contact with skin.

If you want the closest thing to a live visual experience of how lipstick is made, since most cosmetic companies are not fond of having visitors, a good place to go is a crayon factory. The Crayola Company in Pennsylvania gives regular tours. The lipstick-making process is very similar to the crayon-making process, as well as that of making candles.

M•A•C founder Frank Toskan describes making lipstick as like making a souffle, in that it's a process of getting the temperatures and timing just right. It is also like baking a cake, in that you can make a cake from artificial ingredients, or one from natural or more expensive ingredients—it's the same thing in the end on the outside, but what's inside, in the ingredients, is what makes the difference.

A VERY ELEMENTARY GUIDE TO THE PROCESS OF MANUFACTURING A LIPSTICK:

Milling/grinding: With the aid of a three-roller mill, pigments are dispersed in a wetting agent (usually castor oil), and the mixture is ground and formed into a thick "slurry," until there is a uniform mixture and all particles are extremely fine. Waxes are added for texture and to maintain stiffness. Oils, lanolin, and esters are added for specific formula requirements. The finer the mix, the better and more uniform the color.

The mixture is put through a temperature-controlled heating stage. Steamed jackets are used to melt the waxes, paraffins, and fats, causing them to dissolve in the oil, and form a homogeneous liquid in which the coloring ingredients are suspended.

Molding/assembly: The hot liquid is then poured into cold metal molds where it solidifies, and is further chilled. The bullet is then removed (when it is cold, so its shape does not distort). There will then be a dwell time, where it sits (maybe 2–4 minutes).

Flaming: The lipstick bullet is placed into a metal case, then put through a flame, such as a Bunsen burner, for about half a second to create a smooth and glossy finish, further shine, and remove imperfections.

LIPSTICK CAULDRON QUESTIONS AND ANSWERS

1. **Q**uestion: Is the French lipstick you buy at Macy's in New Jersey the same lipstick that's sold on the Champs-Elysées?

Answer: Not necessarily. Many French lipsticks are made not only in France, but in other factories around the world as well. Where on the planet you buy the lipstick will determine whether or not it was made in France, or some other very un-French place. Guerlain is one French product that, no matter where you buy it, will always have been made in France.

2. **Q**uestion: Is the rumor true that some lipsticks are made with squashed bugs?

Answer: Yes, it's true: Your lipsticks *may* include crushed, dried cochineal beetles—which for centuries have been used to create a brilliant or dark red.

3. **Q**uestion: Is it true that fish are used in lipstick?

Answer: Sort of. Frosted, pearly lipsticks include mica, iron oxides, and titanium dioxide. But when these lipsticks were first made in the 1960s, it was fish scales that were used. As a side note: Go gentler with your frosted lipsticks—they are more brittle and tend to break, due to the new nonfish ingredients used in their making.

4. **Q**uestion: How much does it cost to make a lipstick?

Answer: It was estimated at one point in lipstick history that the actual cost of a single wax bullet was one cent, with the manufacturing costs somewhere between three and five cents. It's the advertising and distribution that we're all paying for. One industry source estimates the profit in lipstick to be about ten dollars to every twenty-five cents of cost. According to Andrew Tobias in the book *Fire and Ice,* the retail price of Revlon's Lustrous Lipstick in 1962 was $1.10, while the actual cost was 9.6 cents.

5. **Q**uestion: Are different ingredients used for different kinds of lipsticks?

Answer: Yes. The ingredients vary according to finish (gloss, frost, matte) and coverage (sheer, opaque). Matte lipsticks usually have shorter ingredient listings than the frosted ones. Crayons will include more wax (for the extra-solid body). Lipsticks made by companies who attest to using their conscience when making ingredients will usually have a shorter ingredient list (kind of like those ads we used to see for all-natural versus not-all-natural ice cream). But as with ice cream, a lot of ingredients are the same thing whether they're identified by a name that sounds more politically correct to the layman's ear, or by a more technical name. For example: Tocopherol is the same thing as vitamin E. Butylated Hydroxytoluene can just be "anti-oxidant" or "preservative." Caprylic/Capric Triglyceride, if reworded in the appropriately correct form of cosmetic lingo, can be described as something close to coconut oil.

6. **Q**uestion: What constitutes an "all-natural" lipstick?

Answer: All-natural lipsticks, or as some call them, politically correct lipsticks, use vegetable rather than animal bases and oils, and no petrolatum. Two of the most natural coloring agents are *annatto* (a vegetable dye, creating yellow to pink colors, taken from tropical trees, and also used in baked goods) and *alkanet root* (red in color, extracted from an herblike tree root grown in the Mediterranean, which is also used to color wines). Among the Food and Drug Administration's approved colors, the safest colors are considered to be the FD&C colors (which means they are safe for food, drugs, and cosmetics) rather than D&C colors (which are only safe for drugs and cosmetics). More "natural" lipsticks are almost always softer in consistency, and are mostly available in lighter colors. Take more care watching the freshness of these lipsticks, in the same way you would with natural foods low in preservatives.

7. **Q**uestion: How do you read a lipstick label? What do all those nutty technical and chemical words mean?

Answer: Here're some of the ingredients you will commonly see on a box of lipstick and what they are:

Acetylated Lanolin Alcohol: An emulsifier and emollient, which is used as a water-resistant film (it is considered a better water repellent than plain lanolin). It produces a velvety texture.

Ascorbyl Palmitate: This salt of ascorbic acid is employed as a preservative/antioxidant and prevents rancidity in lipsticks.

Beeswax: Obtained from honeycomb, beeswax is used as a thickener, emulsifier, and stiffening agent. The color can vary from a light amber to a dark brown, depending on the flowers the bees brought home. Beeswax is practically insoluble in water (have you ever noticed lipstick doesn't adhere well to wet lips?).

BHA: (Butylated Hydroxyanisole) An antioxidant/preservative. It has a faint odor.

BHT: (Butylated Hydroxytoluene) An antioxidant/preservative. It has a faint odor.

Benzophenone: There are approximately twelve different benzophenones, so you will see them listed with a number after them. Used as a fixative, this white flaky solid has a roselike scent.

Bisabol: A myrrh-type of gum resin, from African trees.

Bromo Acid: A common coloring agent in lipstick, otherwise known as D&C Red No. 21.

Butylparaben: An antifungal preservative.

Calcium Lake: Used as a whitener.

Candelilla Wax: An herbal wax, in a yellow to light brown color, obtained from the scales of a reedlike plant found in Mexico and Texas. It's used alone or along with other waxes in order to harden them.

Caprylic/Capril Triglyceride: Derived from coconut oil, this oily substance is used to keep moisture in the skin, and for texturizing.

Carmine: A natural red color made from the dried body of a female beetle (cochineal), generally found in South America, Mexico, and Central America, that live on various cactus.

Carnauba Wax: A yellow wax taken from the leaves of Copernica cerifera, a tree grown in Brazil, and referred to there as "the tree of life."

Castor Oil: (Palm Christi Oil) A plant oil, from the seed of the castor-oil plant, used as an emollient and water-binding agent. When dried, it forms a tough shiny film. More than half of the lipsticks made in the U.S. use formulas that include a sizeable percentage of castor oil. Ingesting large amounts of castor oil has been found to possibly cause intestinal congestion though in small doses it has been used for centuries as a medicine. Castor oil has been around forever. In some 4,000-year-old

Egyptian tombs, archaeologists have uncovered castor seeds.

Ceramide: A fatty acid.

Ceresin: This wax is a petroleum product obtained from the mineral ozokerite through a process of bleaching and refining. It is tan in color and is a higher grade of paraffin.

Cetyl Lactate: Used as an emollient and texturizer. It improves the texture and overall feeling of a lipstick.

Esters: This is the organic equivalent of salt. It is formed from an acid and an alcohol, by eliminating water. They are often used as fragrance.

Ethylparaben: (See *Parabens*)

Fatty Acids: In lipsticks, you will not usually see "fatty acid" on the ingredients list. It will appear under its other names, and by the specific types of fatty acid being used. The most commonly listed and used fatty acid in makeup is stearic acid. Fatty acids help keep moisture in the skin.

Iron Oxides: Often referred to as "jeweler's rouge" or "rust." Among the colors derived from iron oxides (iron combined with oxygen) are ocher, sienna, red, brown, orange, and yellow—depending on their purity and the amount of water used.

Isopropyl Lanolate: Used in many cosmetics as an emollient, lubricant, and thickening agent. It gives a high gloss.

Isopropyl Myristate: A fatty compound used as a thickening agent and emollient, and to reduce the greasy feeling caused by other ingredients.

Isopropyl Palmitate: Used as an emollient and texturizer, it is obtained from animal fat and plant oil, palm oil, Japan wax, and Chinese vegetable tallow. Also called Palmitic Acid.

Kaolin (china clay): Often this is the first ingredient listed in *matte* lipsticks. This white clay helps absorb oil, and is used in many cosmetics for its astringent and dehydrating properties.

Lakes: These are solid dye forms that are created when a soluble, liquid color is mixed with an insoluble powder, such as aluminum, calcium, or barium potassium. The color is then made insoluble.

Lanolin: A yellow, fatty secretion from the oil glands of sheep and wool is used as an emulsifier, base, and lubricant for dry skin. Once Hazel Bishop popularized the modern lanolin-based lipstick, it became a major ingredient in most manufactured lipsticks. Several forms of lanolin often appear on ingredients listings: lanolin oil, lanolin alcohol, acetylated lanolin, and hydroxylated lanolin.

Methylparaben: (see *Propylparaben*)

Mica: Used as both a lubricant and as a coloring, this shiny mineral provides sparkle.

Microcrystalline Wax: These are plastic materials obtained from petroleum.

Mineral Oil: A liquid mixture, obtained from petroleum, which keeps moisture in the skin.

Myristyl Lactate: Used as an emollient. (See *Fatty Acids* and *Esters*)

Ozokerite: A natural waxlike material, used as an emulsifier and thickening agent, reputed to have a terrible odor.

Parabens: Used as a preservative and antimicrobial.

Paraffin: A waxy, crystalline mixture obtained from wood, coal, or petroleum, used as a thickener.

Petrolatum: Some companies will not use petrolatum products, going so far as to state in their advertising that they are made from the same stuff that is used to make your car run (petroleum). Some companies do not use it since it's a common allergen. Others claim it is one of the most effective moisturizers—which is its purpose in lipstick.

Phenyl Trimethicone: A silicone oil, employed as a skin protectant, a water repellent, and to give a gloss.

Propylparaben: A preservative; kills bacteria and fungus, and is considered the least irritating preservative used in makeup.

Retinol: A derivative of vitamin A, used to remedy dry skin.

Saccharin: This stuff has been around since 1879. Used as a sweetener in lipstick (estimated to be 300 times sweeter than cane sugar).

Shea Butter: (Karite Butter) An emollient and thickening agent, used to remedy dry skin. It is made from natural fat taken from the fruit of the karite tree or the African shea tree.

Silica: A white powder used to modify texture.

Silicone: Derived from silica, these resins, rubbers, and fluid oils are water repellent and skin adherent.

Stearic Acid: A white, waxlike, crystalline fatty acid used as an emollient and as a base. It is found in butter acids, tallow, cocoa butter, vegetable fats, and animal fats.

Titanium Dioxide: Used mainly as a white pigment. Pinks are created by mixing titanium oxide with various reds.

Tocopherol: (Vitamin E) As used in lipsticks, it's an antioxidant and a preservative.

Colorants: Colorants are almost always at the end of the ingredients list. You will typically see lakes, and the letters FD&C or D&C, followed by a color and a number (this refers to colors approved by the Food and Drug Administration). D&C Red #27 and D&C Red #21 (bromo acid) are common in lipstick.

A WARNING: Some coloring agents that are derived from coal tar (or aniline dyes) have been found in lab tests to cause cancer when ingested. Per the 1960s Color Additive Amendment, such coal-tar additives may now only be used in products intended for external use. If you use eyeshadows or foundations on your lips, be cautious and read the ingredients.

SOME UNGLAMOROUS ORIGINS OF LIPSTICK INGREDIENTS:

Petrolatum: When Brooklyn chemist Robert Chesebrough took off to the region in Pennsylvania where oil was first struck, it was in hope of giving up pharmacy and becoming a petroleum tycoon. But when he noticed a pasty residue that clogged up the workers' drills, his entrepreneurial antennae went elsewhere. What's more, the workers were using the gunk to soothe skin burns and cuts, and, lo and behold, it worked! Chesebrough went back to Brooklyn and struck gold with "petroleum jelly," otherwise known as Vaseline.

Castor Oil: This yellow oil extracted from the castor bean is the earliest recorded laxative. In Egypt it was used by construction workers as a lubricant for stones being moved along wooden rollers.

Lipstick Manipulation Part I:
The Color of a Lipstick

"I had a crush on this guy, and what I did is I went out and found a red-color lipstick and matched it to the color of the shirts he wore. I tried to duplicate those colors on my lips. Eventually, I got what I wanted. Him. A friend did this with lipstick and the color of a guy's car. He was so in love with his car, and she wanted to get his attention the way the car did."

— MARIANNE JONES, MY
NEIGHBORHOOD SUPERMARKET
CHECKOUT CLERK

Lipstick colors are recycled as the seasons pass, and restamped with new names appropriate to the mood of the times. Through the right words, color is manipulated according to whatever pop culture's desires, dreams, and fears happen to be at the moment the tubes hit the shelves. A new name is branded atop a color according to the zeitgeist's flavor of the month.

These recycled colors may have a little more gloss or shimmer or matte. It's the same color, but despite a few adjustments, the only significant thing that changes is the name. And with that new name attached to it, it can suddenly look completely different.

Is it possible that the color you choose says something about you?

There are some powers that color has over lipstick that even the biggest suit with the biggest cigar behind the biggest desk can't manipulate or control. When it comes to color, especially red, there are subconscious and physiological powers at work. And the usual suspect is most often red.

What is it about red? And what is it about red and lipstick?

RED . . . is a color that actually causes physiological changes in the body. It increases blood pressure, respiration rate, and heartbeat. It stimulates the appetite. It's the color with the longest wavelength perceptible to the human eye. Anger causes blood to rush to the brain—thereby the expression "seeing red." Red is the color that gets noticed the most. According to Alexander Theroux in his book *The Primary Colors,* red is the symbolic color of love, magic, revolution, martyrdom, hell, death, and fervor. Theroux writes that it "is the first color of the newly born and the last seen on the deathbed . . . upon merely seeing the color red, the metabolic rate of a human being supposedly increases by 13.4 percent. When subjects viewed a red light—hand-grip strength was being measured—their strength increased almost 20 percent." And red "was the very first color to be designated by name in virtually all primitive languages—the name of Adam, the first man, means, according to ancient Hebrew tradition, both "alive" and "red." A bright, pure red is considered the most passionate color, suggesting the most primal needs.

AND MORE ON RED . . . Purplish and blackened reds have been found to signify emotions and expressions most directly related to sex. Crimson is often associated with active passion. Many darkened reds have been found in color studies to suggest a person's capacity for strong passion—but one that is presently satisfied.

According to Wanda, my neighborhood hairdresser, "In the 1940s, when I was in high school, the bad girls, you know, the ones who did the football team, wore a really deep red lipstick. Nice girls wore the more subdued colors of Tangee lipstick. Older women wore purple-reds."

PURPLE . . . According to the ideas of various color theorists, purple is red made complex. Alexander Theroux, in *The Secondary Colors,* writes that purple is the color of bad magic, uncontrollable anger, a bruise, suffragettes, religious devotion, grief, pride, mystery, enchantment, majesty, and Jezebel.

Purple is a combination of red's virility and blue's spirituality. Purple drives out the pagan force of red. In fairy tales, the evil girl wears dark purple lipstick; the nice girl, pink.

PINK . . . is the color culturally associated with girls. If we think pink, we think health, youth, sweetness. It's the color Princess Diana almost always wore. While red is about blood, pink is about the heart—and is seen as a way to read a female's sexuality or compassion. According to Alison Lurie in *The Language of Clothes,* pinks, which are whitened, paler versions of red, are not so much about passion, but rather are symbolic of affection. As Lurie writes: "A deep rose is the traditional color of romantic love, sexual and emotive. As more and more white (purity, innocence) is added, the sensual content diminishes and finally disappears. Pink is most often worn, in our society, by older women and preadolescent girls, both of whom are supposed to feel strong affection, but not passion." Shocking pink, or fuschia, which is actually a purple, has been called an obscenity of the color.

ORANGE . . . Alexander Theroux writes that orange is "indicative of and supposedly preferred by social types with an agreeable, good-natured, and gregarious personality, glad-handing and salesman-hearty, yammering and bumptious and irrepressible, although it carries the added connotations . . . of fickleness, vacillation, lack of steadiness, and, many even insist, a lack of warmth . . . while at times it may seem thick and impenetrably opaque, it can just as often be lucid. . . . Loudness is orange."

BROWN . . . has always been cheap and easy to produce as a dye. It is the natural color of most fibers and wool, and is often seen in cultures and places of modest means. Brown has been linked symbolically to devotion, humility, asceticism, economic restraint, and intelligent common sense. In the 1990s, brown in lipstick became a popular color and figured in the atonement theory of nineties fashion.

BLUE . . . is associated with distance and sadness. Nietzsche claimed blue and green "dehumanize nature more than any color." It also symbolizes bodily illness and death.

GREEN . . . Like blue, when associated with the body, green symbolizes illness and death. Green also has been popularly associated with rebellion, science fiction, youth, and monsters.

Around the world, certain lipstick colors continuously have more popularity in specific regions. Guerlain has made a few pink lipsticks specifically for sale in Japan, as pink sells very well there. Soft peaches and corals are among the best-selling colors in England. Clear reds sell very well in France.

You'd think there wouldn't be much of a market for the large veil-wearing population of women in the Middle East, but reportedly, underneath those veils, the lips are wearing a dark, reddish black lipstick, the biggest selling colors in this region.

In the 1920s, lipsticks would be available in light and dark, then graduated to light, dark, and medium. Then it moved up to four, then five colors. That was considered a lot. The colors were generally divided into those for brunettes, redheads, and blondes. Later, blonde-browns (Max Factor called them "brownettes") and "silverettes" were added. For more than half of the twentieth century, lipstick apparently suffered from its own form of racism.

Lipstick Manipulation Part II:
Naming Names

"The expression of the soul is translated into two languages: one through vision and the other through speech. The one of vision is born through the eyes while speech is through the lips."

— DIEGO DALLA PALMA

"Man does not live by words alone, despite the fact that sometimes he has to eat them."

— ADLAI STEVENSON[2]

"Words are, of course, the most powerful drug used by mankind."

— RUDYARD KIPLING[3]

"I personally think we developed language because of our deep inner need to complain."

— JANE WAGNER[4]

"In 1938 the cosmetics firm Volupte introduced two new lipsticks. . . . The names of these lipsticks were Lady and Hussy. . . . Women could choose the look of gentlewoman or prostitute—and apparently Hussy outsold Lady five to one!"

—FROM *Hope in a Jar,*
BY KATHY PEISS

In ancient cultures, the name of a thing was often one and the same with *being* that thing. When you were named, you became your name. Particularly within the rites and practice of magic and religion, the name of something was understood to be the object itself. When you ate or drank something with an important name during a ritual, you were combining with the thing/name, becoming it.

Sometimes I think it's the same thing with lipstick. Definitely more so than with any other cosmetic—more so than eyeshadows, or powder, or foundation.

For purposes of magic, the lipstick name may be important in terms of becoming that thing—in either your own mind, or someone else's. Lipstick is an old hand at manipulating words.

I've always been intrigued by the names lipsticks are given and wondered about how they were named.

Estèe Lauder wrote of always making a color *do* something. She usually added a verb to describe a color, or put it at some location where it assumed an activity—like "Cinema Pink." "Flirtation Pink" was a top Lauder seller—and a case in point of color in action, or getting some action.

Revlon was credited early on with not only giving color action, but powers that were deadly or godlike, that made everyone get out of the way while the color did its action.

"Pink Lightning," "Fatal Apple," "Paint the Town Pink," "Where's the Fire?", and "Rosy Future" are among Revlon's greatest hits of lipstick names.

Elizabeth Arden for years created every possible color of pink. Pink was her trademark, and by giving anything a pink association, it suddenly became Ardenized.

Chanel's Hydrabase lipstick ad reads "Treat your lips to the color nature did not dare to give them."

A name can be a reason for its longevity.

In color meetings at BeneFit Cosmetics, they search for names with a sense of humor. In one meeting, joking around, they came up with the name "Ms. Under Stud." After one staff member briefly left the room, they decided to change the name to "Misunderstood," as their first choice might offend. What happened next was that that particular staff member didn't hear about the change of heart, and a shipment of "Ms. Under Stud" went to a major department store in Chicago. "Ms. Under Stud" became a top seller at that store, and the buyer put in an order for 5,000 more. When BeneFit let them know the name was now actually "Misunderstood" the supplier decided that no, sorry, with this new name, they didn't want the color anymore.

Lipstick language is a way that colors can be manipulated to fit the particular vision of the lipstick's creator. At nineteen years old, Poppy King started her lipstick company because she couldn't find the matte lipstick she wanted. Her first color: "Ambition."

Almost always, the color comes first, and then the

name is added on. Less frequently, a color is created for a particular name.

Lipsticks are most often named after foods, fantasy, places, flowers, times of the day, and various female archetypes. A color in the hands of one cosmetic house may have an edgy name, where another house will give you the same exact color with a soft, feminine name.

For the lines of specific makeup artists, it is usually the creator who names the color, while at larger houses, it is by committee or by a person whose job is specifically naming names.

At Prescriptives, there are just a few people on staff whose job it is to name lipsticks. Not only do these people create the names of the lipsticks, but they do all other writing as well—copy, ads, etc.

Kimberly Forrest, a "lipstick namer" at Prescriptives, says she's started to look at everything differently, and almost every experience and activity may end up as a lipstick name. You begin to collect names, and then play off of them. At naming meetings, the group might sit on the floor with pretzels and jelly beans, the colors spread out before them, with names they collected written on cards. The word cards are then moved around and placed next to different colors, until the right colors end up with the right names.

SOME OF THE METHODS OF CREATING NAMES:

WHAT EMOTION OR PLACE DOES A COLOR EVOKE? The cosmetic company Tony & Tina uses chakra color theory in naming their lipsticks. Colors are named according to the emotion or need they evoke or fulfill. According to cofounder Cristina Bornstein, "We wear colors we crave." If you stare at a color, it will evoke a certain sensation, feeling, mood. In choosing color names, she will look closely at a color to see what it evokes.

Brown, she says, is a grounding color, the color of intelligence and common sense. Tony & Tina's browns are named "Intelligent" and "Courageous." Pink is "Loved." Cherry red is "Vital."

THE COLOR IS THE PLACE: At Uni Cosmetics, lipsticks are named for cities and countries. When you think of a place, what does that place look like? Partners Valli O'Reilly and Brooke Hargrove will also look closely at a color, then decide which place the color evokes. Most often, they both make the same decision. "Milan" is a pretty, sheer berry. "New York" is dark, plum, matte, sophisticated, and modern. "Malibu" is a clear, bright pink.

EVOCATIVE/CREATIVE APPROACH: M·A·C's Frank Toskan explains that their colors are created by a group of makeup artists, and that once again, the naming process is a matter of colors being associated with words that come to mind. A purple will be looked at, and someone might mention it looks like cellophane. It looks like plastic. Then the word comes—"Plastique." Or a color is looked at and someone will say, "Look at that color, that looks like ecstacy"—and there's your name. Naming colors is an evocative process. Look at the color—what do you see? The way Toskan describes it, it almost sounds like a jazz riff—where the process of naming evolves from various words, colors, and images, inspiring the next—until you end with the final, perfect note.

Most of M·A·C's colors are created as part of a "color story" (as is the practice at many cosmetic houses), where all the colors will evolve around a particular theme or idea. "Abstract" was part of a launch that was about being experimental and breaking rules. The color and the name delivered the message that we can break rules if we want.

HONORARY AND MEMORIAL LIPSTICKS: Many cosmetic companies will create colors with a particular person in mind. Manic Panic created a funky purplish brown, "Gorilla Rose," in memory of a performance-artist friend who wore huge platform boots, see-through plastic tuxedos, and shaggy, spikey brown wigs. "He lives on in the color," say Manic Panic's creators Tish and Snooky.

At Stila, Jeanine Lobell creates colors for her girl-friends. The colors are mixed by her at home to capture and evoke the particular style of the women she knows. "Cynthia" was created for Cynthia Rowley. Beyond her posse of girlfriends, "Piaf" was created in honor of singer Edith Piaf. "Esme" was inspired by the hero of a J. D. Salinger short story. She also creates colors that are inspired by her children and some of their four-year-old friends, such as "Carver" and "Anabella." *Style* is the key to the Stila lipstick—her lipsticks were created for people she knows who aren't necessarily makeup hounds, but who have a specific and unique style—and that style is captured within the color of the lipstick.

At Lorac, Carol Shaw makes lipsticks that are originally created for specific celebrity clients, including Winona Ryder, Kim Basinger, Angelica Huston, and Nicole Kidman. The first Lorac lipstick came about as a fluke, when Shaw created a lipstick for Farrah Fawcett as an option to replace the lipstick Farrah normally wore that had been recently discontinued. While the lipsticks are in some respects tributes to these women, they also act in a sense as guides to the buyer—if your coloring is similar to that particular star, it might be a good lipstick for you.

Diego Della Palma's "Novecento" lipsticks are made with 1950s film and music icons in mind, using a formula from the fifties used for TV, theater, and opera. One dark red was created to duplicate the one worn by Maria Callas.

Laura Mercier created "M" for Madonna for her work in the film *Evita*. At M•A•C, "Roz" was created for an employee by that name who had big, rosy lips.

FACE Stockholm names their pencils after various employees at their company. Among those employees immortalized in a pencil: Jessica, Tatyana, Cristina, Josephine, Kiki, and Barbro. The pencil "Greco" is named after Gary Greco, the resident makeup artist at the FACE Stockholm Soho boutique.

LIPSTICKS INSPIRED BY MOVIES: François Nars uses what he calls "a magical rather than literal approach," creating colors after both places and movies. "I am always inspired by magical and exotic places, songs, the essence of classic films and the actresses or the fantasy of faraway places that make you dream. When a woman chooses a NARS lipstick, I want her to dream, to feel the magic of old Hollywood or these places. For *Cabaret*—I created the best burgundy lipstick to reflect the mouth from the film. It had great style. It reminds me of Berlin in the 1930s."

Even black-and-white films inspire lipstick colors. Nars says that his lipsticks "Scarlett Empress" and "Shanghai Express": "remind me of the old black-and-white films of Dietrich, and the darkest, richest reds, that even though the film was black and white, you get the feeling that the girl had this very lush red mouth. The color is not what the movie is about, it just makes you feel the essence of the film. . . . 'Jungle Red' is from the film *The Women* with Joan Crawford. You never saw the color red in the film, but you can imagine that it was the clearest, vivid red."

THE TECHNICAL APPROACH: For his shocking pink lipstick, "Schiap," Nars wanted to create the exact color of the cover of Elsa Schiaparelli's memoir, *Shocking Life*. "I searched everywhere for her autobiography . . . because it is bound in her signature shocking pink. I had every book dealer looking for it, and when they found it, I took it to my labs to match the cover, and that is how I created the lipstick."

M•A•C's "Wuss" was made for the designer Wynn Smith who wanted a color that represented his collection. "Blade" was made for Matsuda. Urban Decay's "Bruise" was formulated to match the color of a skin bruise.

LIPSTICKS WITH A SENSE OF HUMOR AND THE LINE-UP APPROACH: At BeneFit Cosmetics, Jean Danielson explains that "naming is random and has nothing to do with reality. We think sexy and funny. We just line them up. We have our color people. We go one color at a time. They do a thumbs-up or -down. We don't ask why. It's either yes or no or yes yes." Many of her names are thought of while she's driving in the car—thus, such colors as "But Officer" and "Sideswipe."

While colors are stamped with different names by different companies, you will notice that colors do evoke some similar images at a number of separate companies. **Dark, reddish browns** are almost uniformly given names that denote urban places, darker emotions, or intense forms of music.

Medium browns are often named after intuitive states of mind, or positive emotions.

Purples are most often named after mystery, distance, and faraway things, things that are difficult to see or comprehend. Chanel's "Phantom" and Urban Decay's "Plague" are somewhat similar colors.

Darker purples are very often named after sexually mysterious subjects, such as "Vamp" and "Siren."

Lighter browns are often evocatively named for skin and touch.

Urban Decay chooses colors that rhapsodize the urban landscape. Some of their copy reads: "Smoggy skies, the pallor of skin that never sees the sunlight . . . a golden-brown roach, mildewed subway tunnels . . . a gash . . . a shattered windshield." According to creative director Wende Zomnir, "We like to look at something that may or may not be beautiful (like a rusting fire escape), and see the beauty within."

Zomnir explains that by wearing some of their lipsticks which come in less extreme colors (others have more out-there colors), the edge you get is from the name rather than the look.

Urban Decay garnered some attention with names such as "Bruise," "Ozone," "Shattered," "Vapor," "Gash," "Smog," "Asphyxia," "Acid Rain," and "Plague." While some of these color names may seem a bit edgy or shockingly bold, get a load of some of the names given to colors during the Renaissance in England: Beggar's Grey, Rat, Horseflesh, Soppes-in-Wine, Puke (a dirty brown), Sad (a gray), Turkey, Blod, Popinjay, Plunket,

Rat's Colour (only for the poor), Sheep, and Popinjay (green).

If we were to put some of these colors to work as liprouge, you might admire a woman's lovely shade of Incarnate, Strammel (1575), or Lustie-Gallant (a light red). A harlot may have worn Sangyn (a deep bloodred), and I bet a madwoman wore Friar or Croyde. When you died, your lips turned Milk and Water (bluish white).

During Mary Tudor's reign, Old Medley was a favorite red, a good choice for the lips. Some colors were made official in England by the order of King Edward VI, such as Murrey (a mulberry), and Edward's favorite color, Raw Flesh, which he had named in 1547.

Some good ones from 1577 include: Goose-turd (yellowish green), The Devil in the Head, and Pease-porrige.

Names catalogued from 1580–1620 include: Scratch face, Beans-blue, Ape's Laugh, Smoked Ox, Ox-Blood, Fading Flowing, Merry Widow, Resurrection, Kiss-Me-Darling, Hair, Chimney-Sweep, Judas-color, Dying Monkey, Mortal Sin, Ham-Color, and Love-longing.

If you ask me, Elizabethan England could have been *the* Golden Age for naming lipsticks.

Lipstick Manipulation Part III:
The Scent of a Lipstick

"Physicians might, I believe, make greater use of scents than they do, for I have often noticed that they cause changes in me, and act on my spirits according to their qualities."

— MICHEL DE MONTAIGNE[5]

Is there a particular allure to the scent of a lipstick?

When non-lipstick wearers smell a lipstick, the first thing they usually say is, "that reminds me of my grandmother" or "that reminds me of my mother."

Fragrance in lipstick has one major job: acting as a mask. The mask often changes with the decades according to the scent of the ingredients it needs to cover.

Most lipstick perfumes aren't really perfumes but flavors. Perfume itself will give the lipstick a creepy taste. Have you ever sprayed your wrist with your favorite cologne, and then tasted it? Not good, is it? Lipsticks are scented with flavors, such as real or artificial strawberry, orange blossom, vanilla, or cherry.

When twenty women were asked to smell different lipsticks and choose which one they liked best, seventeen of them chose the same scent: vanilla.

Frank Toskan, creator of M•A•C Cosmetics, explains that vanilla not only has a great fragrance, but also acts as a natural freshener, and is the least sensitizing ingredient.

Vanilla has a long history as a calming agent. Vanilla aroma is given to cancer patients before receiving chemotherapy. Vanilla has also been used throughout history as an aphrodisiac and a mood elevator.

At the house of Guerlain, Guerlinade, the vanilla base note used in every Guerlain perfume from Shalimar to Jicky to Samsara, is in the lipsticks as well, evoking the glamour and elegance of the expensive perfumes.

Vanilla also evokes the scent of a dessert or cake batter. Since lipstick is often the last thing a woman applies, it becomes like a dessert at the end of a meal.

Rose water is another popular scent used in lipsticks. This is the fragrance reportedly used in Chanel and Lancôme lipsticks, and it too has a medicinal track record. In 1875, it was used in psychiatric hospitals to treat victims of nervousness. No wonder a woman puts lipstick on before she leaves the house as a way to feel put together and strong.

Tish and Snooky, the sisters who opened the first punk rock shop in America, and the creators of Manic Panic Cosmetics, have a large collection of antique lipsticks and say that you can "smellulize" the past through different tubes of lipstick. The scent of a Yardley Slicker lipstick will immediately take you back to the 1960s. Tish and Snooky can describe different periods of their lives through the scents of the lipsticks, starting with the Avon samples their Aunt Madeleine brought them to play with as children. The scent "Liquid Rouge" is used in Manic

Panic's "Vampire Red"—this is the scent that nostalgically reminds them of the lipsticks they could buy from vending machines at truck-stop ladies' rooms in the 1960s—an era when lipsticks were a roadside emergency necessity.

Just One More Thing Before We Send It Out . . . Putting the Wax in the Case, and The Art of Making It Click

As opposed to the twist-up lipsticks that dominate today, the first modern lipsticks were pushups. Usually, there was a little metal lever on the side of the tube, which would be pushed up or down to bring the wax out or back in. To see the inner workings of the twist-up tube, cosmetics company Shu Uemura makes clear plastic vials. On the other end of the spectrum, Shu Uemura also offers vials, created by the designer Georg Jensen for a price of $1,500, that come with a lifetime supply of liprouge. Guerlain's cases are created by the designer Robert Granai, and they've also made cases that recreate an enamel box once owned by Marie Antoinette. But the Golden Age of the lipstick tube is far behind us.

During the 1930s–1950s, lipstick vials became full-blown production numbers. Compacts took on double or triple functions, as cases for lipsticks as well as other makeup, money, or cigarettes. Compacts came with wrist straps. Hudnot made a compact that came with a seventy-nine-page biography of Madame du Barry. Some lipsticks were attached by a chain to a crucifix, whistle, or keychain. Wartime lipstick cases in the 1940s included an emergency flashlight in case of blackout. Perhaps in response to the shortages of war, and the need for women to horde their lipsticks, many compacts that were made came disguised as something else—binoculars opened up into compacts for powder and lipstick, Eastman Kodak made compacts in the shape of cameras that, when opened, revealed the secret female equipment inside. But sadly, those days are gone.

You'd think there wouldn't be much to the vial today. But when it comes to lipstick, some things that you would never think of are more important than you'd know.

For example, for the people who make them, one very important feature of the lipstick case is the sound it makes when clicking shut. In a 1995 *Harper's Bazaar* article, the methods of going about finding just the right click for a lipstick case was investigated. The sound of the lipstick case clicking shut has a sound of finality—as opposed to the click of the compact, which is gentler—and a different kind of good-bye.[6]

Guerlain's creative director Anton-Philipe Hunger says, "We didn't want our lipstick to click so loudly that it would draw attention to a woman who's touching up in public." Guerlain test-clicked between ten and twenty lipsticks before choosing a soft metallic sound.

Lancôme's rep calls their lipstick good-bye snap "a definitive, well-engineered click."

Givenchy's Olivier Echaudemaison calls theirs "a heavy click, more metallic than plastic."

And for Clinique's Jim Nevins: "I think of my mother shutting her purse with a resounding snap, as if to say, 'We're out the door.'"

CHAPTER SIX

HOW TO BUY A LIPSTICK

Dealing with the Drug Dealers at the Mall: An Intimidation Manual

"In the factory we make cosmetics, in the store we sell hope."

— CHARLES REVSON[1]

"When you are thwarted and bad-tempered, a different lipstick has, in a less expensive way, the soothing effect of a new hat."

— *HARPER'S BAZAAR,* 1935

Studies have shown that shopping for a lipstick is the one thing women do together when they reach a certain level of intimacy in a relationship, and this experience acts as a roadmark of their closeness and trust.

"When a woman goes out to buy a lipstick, it's as much fun as sex," says BeneFit Cosmetic's Jean Danielson. "Like hide and go seek. It's play. It has an immediate impact on you. There's a great escapism in purchasing lipstick. Also, it's like a form of locker-room entertainment—'I dare you to find me the right lipstick.' Once you show them a good lip, all of a sudden they're on your side. To find the right lipstick for a woman, I look at what she's wearing. Read her body language. I'll never ask a woman what she likes. I'll guesstimate. I'll choose something ten degrees away from what lipstick she's wearing, so she'll feel a little more sexy, but not 'out there.' Just a little left of center, but still inside where they are. I think what they want is this— 'make me a little different, but don't scare me.' You know, like a librarian who's a little left of center. If she's got on a vampy color, I'm not going to show her a tangerine. She's given me the information I need. Or, if she's not wearing any makeup, often if you look at the clothes—if it's Prada or Polo or Donna Karan, you can estimate her on the lipstick chart. Then you go a little left of what she has on. Women know what they like. When you're at the counter, you read a woman's body language. You sit her down, you say, 'Hey, I'm going to show you a great lip!' You put it on, and they say, 'How did you know?' and I say 'I can tell you who you are.'"

My friend Ruth says that shopping for lipstick is a primal need.

Shopping in general is part of that primal need to hunt. My friend Tanya says hunting down the perfect lipstick is part of the never ending, never quite attainable quest for femininity.

But while you're out on your prowl, there are some things you should know in order to make the hunt a little bit more pleasant. After all, a Neanderthal woman wouldn't have left the cave unaware of the discomforts and dangers lurking in the deep, dark woods, and neither should you. That's why I've put together a small yet handy Intimidation Manual to take with you when you go out hunting.

Dealing with the Drug Dealers at the Mall: A Lipstick Hunter's Survival & Field Guide

Makeup counter people are often referred to as the used car salespeople of retail.

With regrets, I agree.

If you disagree, try this sociological experiment:

Someday, when you have nothing better to do, go from store to store and makeup counter to makeup counter. Mill around unassumingly. Pretend you're waiting for someone, just browsing. Count how many times you observe a buyer's body change while they're at the counter. See how many times you observe Academy Award-winning moments of intimidation. My friend Ruth did this experiment over a three-hour period and counted seventeen moments. I think that number is low. She must not have been paying attention.

Here's another sociological experiment you can try when you have nothing better to do:

Put a washcloth in your bag, then go from store to store, and counter to counter, and see what kind of makeover they give you. Nine out of ten times the lady behind the counter will paint you up to look just like herself. Eight out of ten times she'll tell you that *now* you look good, and hint that when you first came up to her counter, your appearance broke her heart.

But we're not the first in history to be battling Lipstick Intimidation.

The makeup lady with the intimidating touch has a long and complex history.

Cosmetic vendors through time have almost always had the stamp of Quack-Fly-By-Night-Charlatan upon their heads.

And yet, we keep coming back for more.

Before we get into the helpful hints of the Intimidation Manual, let's take a quick walk down the makeup aisles of the past:

In the Sumerian marketplace of 3,000 B.C., a salesman would show his wares, sing about them, then do a few tricks. Not too unlike today, really. If you were in his way, he might make you part of the act, anointing you the butt of a good joke before the crowd.

In Ancient Egypt, shoppers stocked up with products for the afterlife. The intimidation we know today must have been nothing compared to the intimidation factor associated with buying the wrong products for your tomb, and possibly going through eternity lacking, looking tacky, and maybe pissing off the gods in the meantime as well.

In the Middle Ages, you could get your lipstick ingredients at the workshops of the cosmetic makers or at the pharmacy. But if you couldn't afford that route, you'd have to rely on the itinerant merchants hobbling about in the streets and alleys in the ranker districts. There was just one small problem—you had to buy your products before the merchant got attacked and thrown in jail on suspicion of witchcraft. Talk about a shopping headache.

In the 1300s, women of power and money had lotions and potions made for them by alchemists. The makeup was applied to their faces as the alchemist sang a spooky mystical incantation. (And you thought you were under the spell of the lady at the department store counter.)

Common peddlers wandered the countryside during the Renaissance, making stops at rural fairs to play upon the crowd's superstitions in order to make a sale. If you bought their product, then surely that horrible thing associated with a given superstition wouldn't happen to you. But once again, the crowd usually decided at some point that the vendor was a sorcerer, and once they did, it was all over for him, as well as for you and your chance in line.

A favorite evil makeup lady of history is the nineteenth century's Mrs. Sarah Rachael Levenson (better known by her more intimidating, mysterious name: Madame Rachael). Among Madame's items for sale was a best-selling, exotic lip product called "Chinese Leaves." But the real exotic properties of her operation went further inside the building—her House of Beauty was actually a front for a brothel, as well as the front for a lucrative blackmail and jewelry theft business.

Among the makeup-selling techniques that Helena Rubinstein popularized and perfected is this now standard intimidation technique: 1) Greet customer with a charming smile, 2) Touch her face, 3) Let smile crumble into an expression of pity, 4) Shake head sadly, 5) In a soft voice, say something to the effect of: "How sad. Such a beauty, and such terrible skin." Usually that was all she needed to do to insure a sale. She also designed her salons to evoke the look and atmosphere of a quiet confessional, where women could secretly confess their shame. Helena would then exonerate them by selling them a cure.

Pharmacists also reluctantly took on the job of makeup salesmen in the nineteenth and early twentieth centuries. In the early 1900s, Max Factor secretly placed three of his top sales executives behind the counter of a drugstore, disguised as clerks, where they gathered spy data on the selling techniques and atmosphere of trust the U.S. pharmacy counters were famous for.

During WWII, the British lipstick salesperson was akin to a drug dealer in the street—once the lipstick business became a full-fledged bootleg operation.

THE INTIMIDATION MANUAL'S QUICK POCKET GUIDE TO WARDING OFF MAKEUP-COUNTER EVIL:

I've heard women whisper that the lipstick lady is a necessary evil, like the drug dealer on the street—who you're forced to do business with, humiliation and degradation notwithstanding.

Between the people who spray perfumes at you, and the one who screams out the ultimate humiliation: "Can I give you a makeover?" walking down the cosmetic aisles can make you feel like a leper wandering the streets of a medieval village.

When a lipstick salesperson is creepy, you feel as if you're under their spell. You feel you can't walk away. You shake your head and nod and feel stupid, but somehow you sit there and take it.

HERE'S SOME ADVICE FROM THE PROS ON WARDING OFF INTIMIDATION:

ADVICE FROM KEITH RICHARDS:

"Cats would come around try to sell you stuff . . . My high for a while was watching their faces when I said no, when they couldn't make a sale . . . I 'd watch their faces . . . that would be my high." (That's Keith—talking not about lipstick salespeople—but about drug dealers in the days after he gave the stuff up. But I personally think it's great advice to ward off makeup-counter intimidation and evil.)[2]

ADVICE FROM PAULA BEGOUN, COSMETIC CONSUMER SPECIALIST:

✔ **If you feel intimidated, walk away.**

✔ **Don't be afraid to ask for samples.** Good salespeople know it's okay to ask, and that they have a better chance at a sale if you try the stuff at home.

✔ **Know that at most stores, you *can* return a lipstick.** If you feel you are not sure, you can always change your mind later. "Returning products and explaining our preferences and complaints is a great way to educate manufacturers. We can tell them what we think, but companies . . . listen better when it affects their bottom line."[3]

ADVICE FROM MY AUNT HARRIETT, LIPSTICK-SHOPPING MASTERMIND AND AMATEUR CRIMINAL:

🖊 FIRST: KNOW THEIR TRICKS BETTER THAN THEY DO:

🖊 **If a color seems wrong for you but the salesperson insists too strongly** that it's fabulous, it may be that their supervisor has instructed them to sell as many of a new color or product as possible.

🖊 **Remember the commission factor.** You're doing them a favor by giving them business, not the other way around.

🖊 **Know that they may be operating via the manipulative instructions of their training manual.** Case in point: Aunt Harriett stole a manual on selling techniques from a makeup counter when no one was looking. Here's some of what was inside:

"Never tell a customer you are sorry they chose not to buy or let them think it made you mad. Give a sample as 'our gift' to think about at home. In telling about a product, do not let your speech go past twenty-five seconds; be sure to keep your eyes on customer and your hand on the product the whole time. Slowly pull the product closer to your body (heart region) as you speak. Do not ever turn your back. How you say hello will make or break the sale. Say hello with voice *and* eyes. Always introduce other products that will make the one they want work better. Always give them a reason to return. Always have them leave thinking about what more they can get from you."

Here's some bonus information that Harriett culled from eavesdropping at the drugstore:

According to a marketing executive at one makeup house, women feel most comfortable when they are fifteen feet inside a store, with a turn to the right. This is where companies want to place their product, as they want to get the woman at the spot in the store where she is most comfortable. That is where you will usually see the top lines.

ONCE YOU HAVE GOTTEN PAST, OR MASTERED MAKEUP-COUNTER INTIMIDATION, HERE'S SOME GENERAL MAKEUP-COUNTER ADVICE TO FOLLOW WHEN SHOPPING FOR A LIPSTICK:

YOUR MOUTH WEARS THE LIPSTICK, NOT YOUR HAND: Whenever possible, try colors on your lips. For sanitary application, many counters will have Q-Tips handy. M•A•C began the practice of using alcohol to clean lipstick testers. If you don't want to try it on your lips, test the lipstick on your *inner* wrist. This skin is closer in color to your face.

BE CAREFUL OF REBUYING: We tend to buy the same shades over and over again. Try to find a color a little outside of what you normally have. You can always add it to other colors you already own to alter it. You don't want to have a drawer full of twenty lipsticks in the same color. For the money you're spending, it's better to have several colors, which you can then turn into more combinations.

DON'T BUY ACCORDING TO COLOR AS IT APPEARS ON A PAMPHLET: The color is usually different in print than it is in actuality. However, a good practice is this:

BRING A PIECE OF WHITE PAPER WITH YOU: Generally, you will be trying on various colors on your lips or your hand, and when you go home, they'll have faded and you'll forget all the different colors you tried on. If you bring a few plain white pieces of paper with you, draw on the color, and then write down the name next to it. You will be able to think about it at home, or be able to determine its texture better, its vibrancy, and if it looks too waxy or sheer, etc.

SOME COUNTERS ENCOURAGE TESTING MORE THAN OTHERS: If you like to lounge and play, many boutiques encourage this, and you'll feel more comfortable trying things there than at a counter where the dealer hovers over you and asks you not to sample on the lips. Remember, at a department store, you can try out *all* the counters. Most lines have similar colors, in variation. If you like a lipstick at one counter, you may also find a similar one at another—maybe one that you actually like better.

AVOID MAGAZINE-COVER FRAUD: If you set out to buy a lipstick based on one that is credited as being worn by a model in a magazine photo, particularly on the cover, you may be duped. Although one brand name and color will be credited for the photo, most often what you actually see is the credited lipstick *plus* many other colors that the makeup artist has mixed in.

TEST DRIVE THE COLOR BEYOND THE COUNTER: Wear a color for a few hours to see how it feels, lasts, and looks in different light. Then decide. Fluorescent lights in many stores can drain out the pink and reds in skin, and accentuate the grays and blues, so see how the color looks in daylight.

KNOW WHICH INGREDIENTS YOU ARE BUYING: It is not a crime to ask to see the box before you buy the lipstick so you can read the ingredients. Buying a lipstick where ingredients are not included at all is not a great idea. Many companies who are proud of their formulas will list the ingredients at the bottom of their pamphlets, made available at the counter.

FIND A COUNTER THAT HAS A MAKEUP ARTIST: It's free. If there's a charge, it's redeemable in makeup. This is a great way to learn new techniques, find out what colors look good on you that you might not have thought about before, and to get individual attention from a trained artist. They're also helpful for keeping your fashion current and aware of new trends. Makeup artist Matthew Van Leeuwin (creator of InBeauty Cosmetics), says the way to know a good makeup artist is similar to how you know a good masseuse. You can usually tell in the way the artist's hands touch your face—in the gentleness and care. A good makeup artist deals with you very one-on-one, with sincerity and respect. You will usually know instinctually the ones you trust and the ones you don't.

SOME FURTHER SUGGESTIONS
FROM SOME OTHER PROS:

SOPHIA LOREN SUGGESTS: "On your next trip to buy makeup you cast aside all those rules and try a few shades of red that you never thought of before, just for fun. In my experience, most women get very set in their ways about the shade they wear. . . . But you might be surprised to find that a change in color gives your face a real lift. It is worth a try, and the worst that can happen is that when you leave the store, you look like a little girl who invaded her mother's dressing table and went wild!"[4]

AND HERE'S WHAT JOAN COLLINS SUGGESTS: "Experimenting with cosmetics doesn't mean spending tons of money. The best way to find out what suits you is to ask for a free makeup demonstration at a department store, determine what colors suit you best, then buy the same shades through a less expensive manufacturer."[5]

How Do You Know
a Great Lipstick?

HERE'S WHAT SOME OF THE PROS SAY:

🖌️**LET YOUR HAND DO THE TALKING: RUSSELL PFLUGER, COCREATOR OF ENGLISH IDEAS COSMETICS** explains that drawing a lipstick on the back of the hand is what is called the Payoff. The Payoff is reflective of the amount of pigment in a lipstick, and it's your answer to the quality of the product (pigment is the most expensive ingredient in a lipstick). If you get a full, even cover in one or two strokes—that's a good lipstick. If you have to rub it back and forth several times before you get a sense of the color and coverage, it's a dud.

🖌️**MATTHEW VAN LEEUWIN, CREATOR OF INBEAUTY COSMETICS** also says that drawing the lipstick on the back of the hand will help you see the formula's evenness, strength of pigment, and overall quality. A good lipstick should feel like a drink of water on the skin. It should feel good.

FRANK TOSKAN, CREATOR OF M·A·C COSMETICS: According to Toskan, what makes a good lipstick is what is important to you. A good lipstick should do what it is that *you're* looking for. What makes a good lipstick for one person is not the same for another. The one thing that's of importance for everyone, however, are the ingredients. Good ingredients make a good lipstick. It is important for a lipstick to have properties within it that are good for the skin.

FRANÇOIS NARS, CREATOR OF NARS COSMETICS: "Color and texture make the perfect lipstick. There are a few reasons a woman chooses a lipstick, first because it is a flattering color to her face and second, to create status or the perfect accessory. But a woman should look at the quality of a lipstick as well. It shouldn't be greasy, or it will smudge and feather. Lipstick should be rich with pigment so it holds, it doesn't come off, and you don't have to reapply it all of the time."

CAROL SHAW, CREATOR OF LORAC COSMETICS: Good lipstick feels good on the lips. "It should have a buttery, luscious feeling. If lipstick feels good, it is doing something good for you. Feeling good is what is most important. If you look good, you feel good, and if you feel good, you can do anything."

🖋 **THE SCENT ALSO INDICATES QUALITY—JEAN DANIELSON, COCREATOR OF BENEFIT COSMETICS** says "It should never smell like an old box of crayons. When you put on good lipstick, you smell that soft, almost baby powder fragrance. It's really a smell and a taste together. It should be a pleasant one for you."

🖋 **BOBBI BROWN, CREATOR OF BOBBI BROWN COSMETICS:** "Find a lipstick that looks good on your face when you are wearing absolutely no makeup. This is the magic color that will make your skin, hair, and eyes look their best. . . . When you have found it, you will know." (From *Bobbi Brown Beauty*)

A MEDIUM DOUBLE LATTE FRAPPE CAPUCCINO WITH NONFAT MILK or CHOOSING AND DIFFERENTIATING FROM ALL THE LIPSTICKS OUT THERE:

The choices can be downright dizzying. To give you an example, here is a quick rundown of just some of the lipsticks that were featured within one very thin issue of a major fashion magazine:

Colour riche lipstique; powder lipstick; lip polish; lip conditioner; protective lip tint; lip food; two-toned lipsticks; all-in-one for cheeks lips and eyes; half lipstick–half gloss for when lipstick is too much and gloss is too little; lipstick magic markers; breath-freshening lipsticks; mood balancing lipsticks; nylon-powdered lipsticks for better adhesion; moisture-release lipsticks; lipsticks that have color that continuously renews itself via tiny capsules of time-release pigments; self-renewing lipsticks for every time you press your lips together; fake designer lipsticks that pretend to be your favorite Chanel or Lancôme when you can't afford the real deal; custom-blend lipsticks; half liner half lipsticks; swirl lipsticks; sponge-applicator lipsticks; cellular lip treatments; aromatherapy lipsticks; never-come-off-until-you-want-them-to lipsticks; lipsticks formulated specifically for kissing; lipsticks formulated specifically for honeymoons; lipsticks that a team of thirty scientists worked on; lipsticks that a team of dermatologists worked on.

I think it might be easier if we stick with understanding just a few of the main ones, and at least getting those straight:

MATTE: A flat, opaque and nonshiny cover. Mattes have the strongest colors. Can be drying, but stays on longer than other formulas.

LONG-LASTING: These are advertised as having special formulas high in pigment, and stay on for hours and hours, more than the typical matte. The jury is still out on this claim. These usually have a matte finish, but are also flatter and heavier than the usual matte.

MOISTURIZING/CREAMY: These lipsticks usually feel the best on the lips. They are opaque, have some shine, and most often are strong in color, with good coverage. The moisturizer in these lipsticks is creamy, rather than glossy.

SHEER: Lipsticks that give a translucent, light cover, with a *light shine* thrown in. Recommended for the person who wants *some* color, but also a more natural look.

STAIN: A lipstick with a light trace of color. This is not too different from a sheer, but the focus here is on the trace of *color* staining the lips, whereas the sheer creates more of an effect of colored shine. Both stains and sheers are the most natural-looking lipsticks. As it wears away, is the least likely to leave clumps or lines of color.

SPF-15 LIPSTICKS: SPF-15 (sun protection to level 15) is the sunscreen most often used in lipsticks. Sometimes they're given the name SPF-15 lipsticks, and sometimes the sunscreen is part of the mix but not part of the name.

GLOSS: A heavy, shiny coverage. If it contains a moisturizer, it's Vaseline-based, so that's the feel you'll get. Often, glosses come in a little pot, just like liprouge did in the old days.

LIP CRAYONS: These contain a firmer wax and less oil than regular lipsticks. Crayons often come in the form of a thick pencil (sort of like a thick version of a lip pencil) and require sharpening. They are popular with teenagers because they are very easy to maneuver.

IS THERE A DIFFERENCE BETWEEN BUYING A HIGH-PRICED, OLD-MONEY, ARISTOCRATIC LIPSTICK OR A WORKING-CLASS LIPSTICK FROM THE DIME STORE?

One of the biggest questions in buying a lipstick is whether or not price makes a difference. I'm still trying to figure this one out. Basically, it comes down to what works for you, what you like. Cristina Carlino of Philosophy Cosmetics recommends that "if you find a color and a formula that you like, stick with it!"

A FOOTNOTE TO LIPSTICK SHOPPING: BY THE WAY, HOW DO YOU KEEP UP WITH THE COSMETICS COUNTER? AND WHY DOES IT KEEP CHANGING SO FAST?

One explanation comes from the great egghead book *Dress, Adornment, and the Social Order:* "In the simple folk society, stability instead of change is stressed, for tradition is characteristic in all phases of life. In a complex, industrial society, a strong faith in progress through change permeates all but the most sacred aspects of the society. The emphasis [is] on change. . . . Change in patterns of dress occurs swiftly and is often pursued."

LIPSTICK PLANET: If lipstick shopping around the world, know how to ask for it in their language: **Australian and British:** "Lippy"; **Saudi Arabian:** "AlamRoosh"; **French:** "Rouge à Levre"; **Japanese:** "Kuchi beni"; **Russian:** "Goobah ya pamada"; **Irish:** "Bealdath"; **Chinese:** "Kouhong"; **Spanish:** "Lapiz para los labios"; **Croatian:** "Sminka"; **Swedish:** "Lappstift"; **German:** "Lippenstift"; **Greek:** "Krayion"; **Dutch:** "Laebestift"; **Italian:** "Il Rossetto"; **Hungarian:** "Ruzs"; **Vietnamese:** "Son Moi"; **Haitian:** "Fa"; **Danish:** "Laebestift"; **Finnish:** "Huulipuna"; **Thai:** "Lipsa-dtik."

CHAPTER SEVEN

HOUDINI AND MERLIN'S LIPSTICK AND OTHER TRICKS OF THE TRADE

"Make up is really hot and icky, and if straight men ever really knew what women went through to do it, they'd treat 'em a hell of a lot better."

— TRANSVESTITE PORN STAR
CHICHI LARUE[1]

"Of all the organs of sense, the mouth admits, I believe, of the greatest beauty and the greatest deformity."

— RALPH WALDO EMERSON

"One swipe of lipstick can instantly make a woman look sexier, sweeter, bolder, more rested, more polished, more glamorous, or more put-together."

— BOBBI BROWN[2]

"There is nothing more feminine than putting on a lipstick. It is the mark of a woman. In terms of our fascination with icons of femininity, there is nothing more potent than a lipstick, and the image of a woman applying it."

— POPPY KING, CREATOR OF
POPPY LIPSTICKS

"Well of course it's great to know that given an hour and a gorgeous frock I can do it; I can be fabulous and play the movie star. It's all a question of lipstick."

— ACTRESS KRISTIN SCOTT THOMAS[3]

"If people want to spend their whole lives creaming and tweezing and brushing and tilting and gluing, that's really okay too, because it gives them something to do."

— ANDY WARHOL[4]

"Stand before the mirror when you put on your lipstick and visualize the lips you want. See in the mirror the face you want. The channelled thoughts will help make the right mouth."

— LUCY THE WITCH'S
APPLICATION PHILOSOPHY

"Put on a red lipstick and immediately you're a diva."

— CAROL SHAW

"More than any other piece of makeup, lipstick is the most mood altering."

— JEANINE LOBELL

"Look at the style of Paloma Picasso, red is her trademark. Or the old movie stars and how they created style to begin with. They developed their signature color. I love the way Diana Vreeland wore her lipstick, it was so outrageous but what a great style with so much of her character. It was larger than life, as was she. I think lipstick can easily become a woman's trademark. . . . I think lipstick is the fastest, least expensive fix to the cravings of style."

— FRANÇOIS NARS

"For a single woman, preparing for company means wiping the lipstick off the milk carton."

— COMEDIAN ELAINE BOOSLER[5]

APPLICATION:

"The Golden Rule is that there are no Golden Rules."

— GEORGE BERNARD SHAW[6]

"The tyrant is nothing but a slave turned inside out."

— HERBERT SPENCER[7]

When it comes to lipstick application, do what you like.

My favorite advice from makeup artist Kevyn Aucoin in his books *The Art of Makeup* and *Making Faces* is that the rule to follow is what feels good and looks right to you personally; it is best to follow whatever comes naturally and whatever makes you happy. If you would like to learn more intricate and technical application tools, with the right amount of practice, anyone can do the lips. It's just a matter of practice.

Jeanine Lobell, the creator of Stila Cosmetics offers another good comment of advice in terms of lipstick and makeup application—"If your application takes an hour, it takes you an hour. If it takes you five minutes, so be it. There are no rules. Do what you like, wear what you like, put it on how you like, whether you're eighteen or eighty-one."

Most makeup guidebooks advise ending the makeup routine with the lips, but again, if you want to start with the lips, start with the lips. Makeup artist Matthew Van Leeuwin says, "I sometimes start by just dabbing on a bit of lipcolor to see where it takes the face."

Jeanine Lobell, on the other hand, says that the lipstick is usually the last thing she does, but it's the lipstick that really makes the face. Jeanine says that often when she's doing a client's makeup, sometimes during the process, the client will worry that oh, maybe this is too much, or this is not going to work, but once the lip goes

on, "they get it." Once the lipstick's on, it all comes together.

YOU CAN GO THE FULL NINE-COURSE METHOD IN APPLICATION, OR JUST ROLL THE TUBE OVER YOUR LIPS. THE CHOICES IN APPLICATION ARE MANY, AND THE CHOICES ARE YOURS.

In *Making Faces,* Kevyn Aucoin offers the following techniques for making a great mouth: Line your lips with a
neutral lip pencil, even when you're using a bright lipstick. Not only does this create a much more natural look,
but, Aucoin adds, "if the color fades or is 'chewed off,' the
layer underneath is not a bright orange or red." When applying lipstick, use this *blotting technique:* apply lipstick,
blot lips, apply lipstick again, and blot once more. Use
one sheet at a time of a separated two-ply tissue. "This ab-
sorbs excess oil and leaves the pigment." Aucoin also recommends that *powder* "over the top of the first coat of
lipstick then reapplying will help it last longer." And, for
extra polish to your look, put *foundation* around the area
of the mouth in order to cover facial marks, so it doesn't
look like your lipstick has smudged. It will also give lip
color a boost.

🖌 **LINER AND LIPSTICK TOGETHER:** One
popular way to do the lips is to first fill the lips in
with a liner, and then to draw the lipstick over it.
Or, you can blend the lipstick and the liner together, which usually makes for a very long-lasting
effect.

FULL NINE-COURSE MEAL APPLICA-TION: 1) Put a light foundation on your lips. Use a liquid, as creams run more. 2) Then, draw in lip pencil (a shade similar to your lipstick, or slightly darker, whichever you prefer). 3) Apply lipstick. 4) Blot. 5) Powder the lips. 6) Apply lipstick again. 7) Blot. 8) Touch up the liner again. 9) Add a sealant. The full nine-course application method is used to build up color in the same way the fragrance industry recommends layering perfume— starting with powder, then adding lotion, and then liquid perfume. You can also view the layering of colors in the same way you'd view the bottom notes and top notes of fragrance, by starting with your base-note color, and adding notes of other colors atop that. By putting lip pencil down first you're giving the most matte, nonslippery base to the operation. For longevity, it's good to start with a nonoily formula on which everything else will sit.

NO-NONSENSE APPLICATION: The easiest method is to define, color, and not try to change or correct. Just roll on the lipstick, and leave it at that.

APPLICATION BY USING FINGERS: Place small dots of color in the center of your lips. Then, gently move it with your pinky toward the corners of the mouth. Use just a little bit of lipstick, and the effect is subtle and soft.

THREE-DIMENSIONAL LIPS: Makeup artist Matthew Van Leeuwin recommends, "Make a more interesting lip with more texture. Allow the color to move with the lip." Use this method of layering to create shape. Contour—blend liner into lipstick. To give more shape and three-dimensionality, put a little highlighter in the center of the bottom lip. A good gloss will have three or four pigments in it. It is those subtleties and blends of textures and pigments that you should go for. "What creates interest is that marriage of different shades of texture and color . . . that goes a step beyond just sitting there, it dances on the lips."

✔ **THE WHITE LINE:** A line of white highlighter or gloss just above the cupid's bow of the top lip will give the mouth more attention (this technique is regularly used in fashion and beauty photography).

FINISHING TOUCHES:

✔ **TO GET LIPSTICK OFF THE TEETH:** Put a finger in your mouth, close lips around it, and pull it out.

✔ **STAY AWAY FROM OIL IN FOOD, SUCH AS SALAD DRESSING OR PIZZA** if you're wearing a long-wear lipstick, or any lipstick that you don't want to come off, since oil usually dissolves lipstick.

BLOOD AND FEATHERS:

This is the Number One Fear in the roster of Lipstick Paranoia. Even those two words are supposed to scare you: blood, feathers. Bleeding and feathering. Next thing you think of is tar. Tar and feathering. Punishment for doing the lipstick thing wrong. Use liner to avoid bleeding/feathering, which contains less oil than a lipstick and more wax. Strong wax liners work as a barrier, keeping the lipstick from wandering out beyond the line. Next, use a matte lipstick, which bleeds the least. Vaseline and heavy glosses have a higher tendency to bleed and should be avoided. Clear lip liners are a good choice, as are liquid lipsticks, since they're neither too matte nor too runny, and since the look is gentler, bleeding is less obvious. It is also advised that you avoid waxing the hair on the upper lip, and to bleach the hairs instead, as this down will absorb the moisture that exacerbates feathering.

LIPLINERS:

LIPLINER OPERATIONS: The two main reasons for wearing liner are: 1) to stop bleeding, and 2) it gives the shape of the mouth more definition. To get a softer line, use the *side* of the pencil, rather than the point, or be sure the point is not very sharp. Another way to soften up liner is to follow your liner with a dry lip brush moved along the line you've drawn. If you are a victim of Fear of Lipliners, get past this by putting on liner with light, small strokes on a relaxed mouth (a slow sketch-sketch-sketch approach).

ADVICE FROM A DIFFERENT KIND OF PRO: I was always curious how drag artists were able to do their lipstick so well. To find out, I contacted the dean of Miss Vera's Finishing School for Girls Who Want to Be Boys, the world's first cross-dressing academy. Miss Veronica Vera offers the following advice (which I think is great advice for boys or girls): "In the beginning, it is best that he follows the lip line exactly. As he becomes more sure-handed he can add fullness. . . . It is best to close the mouth and smile so the result will be a happy face and not a droopy mouth. . . . A soft lip pencil is easier to use than a hard one."[8]

MORE LINER/PENCIL APPLICATION TIPS: Makeup artist Adrien Arpel suggests that "If you have trouble drawing a straight outline, put your middle and forefinger on either side of your mouth (fingers forming a *V* shape) and gently stretch. At the same time, stretch your lips over your teeth. Artists know it's easier to draw on a firmly pulled rather than wavy canvas. . . . Start in the center of the top lip, draw a line out to one corner in a nonstop, fluid motion. . . . For the bottom lip, start in either corner and proceed with one nonstop line to the other corner. To assure that the left and right sides of your upper lip will be the same size, draw an X from the top of one side of your cupid's bow to the top of the other to delineate the upper lip. . . ." From *Adrien Arpel's 851 Fast Beauty Fixes and Facts.*)

KEVYN AUCOIN RECOMMENDS starting dark at the corners with your liner and getting lighter as you move inward, fading away until there is almost nothing left at the center of the mouth.

THEN AGAIN, THERE'S ALWAYS THE ANTI-LIPLINER LEAGUE: Not everyone is a fan of the lipliner look. Many women feel intimidated at the makeup counter when the salesperson whips the thing out; and embarrassed when they see the effect. Liner is just one look among many. Don't feel you have to do it. Cristina Carlino of Philosophy Cosmetics, for one, counts among her general lipstick rules: "No coloring outside the lines, and no dark lipliner. It is aging and can be clownish. Furthermore, it causes any asymmetry in the lips to be greatly exaggerated. If you are going to use a liner, match the liner color to your natural lip tone."

THE BRUSH:

IS THE BRUSH FOR YOU? Many women don't like the feeling of a brush, or have trouble maneuvering it, but makeup artists advise using a brush for a professional look, and they claim it makes the lipstick last longer. This may be because the brush works like nail polish—adding one even layer on top of another.

A GOOD BRUSH should be about one-eighth-inch in diameter, of small size, and firm. A sable brush is generally considered the best choice.

- **RETRACTABLE BRUSHES** with a cap are good choices, as they keep the brush clean and can be carried in a handbag.

- **THE FLAT END OF A BRUSH** can be used to make long, fluid strokes and for filling in the full lip area.

- **THE BRUSH'S EDGE OR TIP** can be used for fine lines and small touches.

- **IT IS HELPFUL TO PRACTICE** with a brush on your lips, or on a piece of paper. On a piece of paper you have a more objective look at the mechanics of how it works.

TAKING CARE OF YOUR TOOLS:

- **KEEP YOUR BRUSHES DRY.** Lipsticks, too. Lipsticks are a combination of oil and wax, neither of which mix well with water. A wet lipstick or brush will interfere with smooth application. Clean your brushes every two to three months.

- **MILD SOAP CLEANS BRUSHES WELL.** Just don't soak them—rinse well, and let air dry.

- **REFRIGERATE:** If you put pencils in the freezer for about ten minutes before using them, the point has less of a chance of breaking. If your home is unusually hot in the summer, it is a good idea to put your pencils, lipsticks, and especially glosses in the refrigerator, as they will soften or melt. If you buy lipstick in bulk, refrigerate the ones you are not yet using so they will last longer. If you feel refrigeration is weird, keep lipsticks and glosses in a cool place. Wax melts.

WHEN LIPSTICKS BREAK: Adrien Arpel advises using a "cigarette lighter to slightly melt the bottom of the broken piece and the piece it must adhere to. Attach both pieces and seal the edge of the break with a match or lighter. Remold . . . while the lipstick is still soft. Put it in the fridge until it sets." And, if your lipstick's constantly breaking, "reshape it . . . into a wedge. Cut off the top with an X-Acto knife or razor blade."[9]

A NOTE ON LIPSTICK HYGIENE: Think about how you wash your forks and spoons every time after you use them. Lipsticks should be kept fairly clean too. Obsessive cleanliness isn't necessary. It is recommended, however, that every now and then you clean the bullet with a small amount of alcohol. Another hygiene note: once you notice an odd smell reeking from your lipstick, or if it starts to taste foul, that's your signal that it's gone rancid. This goes for all your cosmetics. Think of it like food going bad in the fridge. As makeup maven Veronica Vera puts it: "You know it's time to retire your lipsticks when they make your lips stick or they begin to smell like crayolas." The life of a lipstick from the time it is opened is estimated at one to two years, but I know a lot of women whose lipsticks have *long* outlived that number. If the color or performance changes, you will know it's time for good-bye. In the meantime, keep them away from heat, strong window light, and steamy bathrooms.

OTHER HAMMERS AND NAILS TO ADD TO YOUR TOOLBOX:

LIP SCRUFFS: This tool, which seems to have been kept a secret for a long time, is similar to a pumice stone. Rubbed against the mouth, it takes off dead skin, and curbs chapping. You can get an inexpensive lip scruff at the Body Shop, or a more sophisticated lip scruff compact at Chanel, at a more Chanel price.

ALTERNATIVES TO A LIP SCRUFF: Brushing your lips with a baby's toothbrush will take off dead skin. It will also temporarily swell your mouth and create a pouty look.

PRIMERS, FOUNDATIONS, AND SEALANTS: If ever there were lip products to make you overly aware of the fact you're *painting,* these are them. Just like the same-named products that you use to paint a house, the primer acts as a base for all the paint to come on top, and the foundation similarly acts as a base for the lipstick.

PRIMERS AND FOUNDATIONS are basically the same thing. Primers can be colored or clear, moisturizing or matte. They are used to hold the lipstick in place for longer periods of time and keep the color truer. Skin-colored primers are used so that the natural color of your lips does not interfere with the color of the lipstick. Clear primers act more as a moisturizing base. For a clear primer, ChapStick is good—it isn't greasy, and will help prevent bleeding. Makeup artists often use a liquid face foundation as a base, but for all-day wear when you may be eating your lipstick, you should be careful of the ingredients in a foundation.

LIP SEALANTS are like the top coats used for nail polishes. A sealant is a transparent cover that will help color wear longer and prevent feathering.

ILLUSIONS

"Reality is the leading cause of stress for those in touch with it."

—JANE WAGNER[10]

CHANGING THE LIPS:

"If God gave you some uneven features, you can redesign your face to some extent," wrote Eternal Lipstick Ambassador Joan Crawford. The mouth is actually the one part of the face that, when it is changed, will most dramatically alter the face in its entirety.

- **For lips that are turned down at the corners,** use a lip liner to draw a little line in an upward tilt at the outside edge of your mouth.

- **A droopy lower lip** can be lessened by using a slightly darker color on that lip, thus drawing attention to the one on top. Place a little gloss on the top lip as well.

- **If you want to make your lips bigger,** use a liner to draw just outside the natural line of your lip. If you want them to look smaller, draw just inside the lip.

- **Dark colors naturally recede or diminish,** making lips look smaller

- **Light colors naturally highlight** and make lips larger.

- **Bright colors** also make the mouth look larger.

THE MOST COVETED ILLUSION—A FULLER MOUTH:

- **MAKING THE ILLUSION OF FULLER LIPS:** This is one of the all-time favorite tips of many makeup artists: Put a dab of gloss in the center of your lower lip, or your upper lip (whichever you choose, it will make that lip look bigger). Most women opt for the bottom—but try both and see which you like better. If not gloss, you can use a dot of golden lipstick at the center.

🖌️**WAY BANDY'S PALE POUTY MOUTH RECIPE:** "Color the lips with a flesh-toned cosmetic pencil. . . . Then rub . . . a fingertip to distribute and blend the color. Use a tissue to blot away excess pigment. . . . Mix a dot of sand beige foundation with a dot of clear lip gloss to make a neutral tone lip color. With lip brush apply to your lips the neutral tone lipcolor that you mixed. Blot excess with tissue. Effect should be a pale, pouty, slightly swollen mouth."

CREATING A LIPSTICK WARDROBE:

"If you are a makeup minimalist, the one must-have after a good SPF-15 moisturizer is a wardrobe of lipsticks."

— MARTINA ARFWIDSON, COCREATOR OF FACE STOCKHOLM COSMETICS

🖌️**IN PUTTING TOGETHER A COLOR WARDROBE, HELENA RUBINSTEIN RECOMMENDS** that "your lipstick collection can be started with one light and one deeper tone lipstick particularly flattering to the skin and the colors you are currently wearing. Then, for corrective modeling, you can add as many new fashion shades as you wish each season. If you wear blues and violets you will want at least one shade with a blue note." (From *My Life for Beauty.*)

✒ **MORE WARDROBE TIPS: BROOKE HAR-GROVE, COCREATOR OF UNI COSMET-ICS** and a veteran of the industry specializing in color, says that with just three lipsticks, one or two glosses, and two pencils, you can create a number of different looks. With a palette, and a general understanding of the color wheel, you can mix together the colors on your own, and you really can get any color you want.

✒ **HAVE BLUE AND WHITE IN YOUR COLOR WARDROBE:** Although on their own they may seen too daring, white and light blue are actually two of the best staples to have in a wardrobe, particularly a white lipstick, since when they are combined with other colors, they create the largest number of varying possibilities. Two other good staples to have are beige and gold.

✒ **TO WORK WITH PURE COLORS:** M·A·C sells pure color pigments in tubes (along with a texture-changing gloss), and with these tools, you can create any color and texture you would like.

WORKING YOUR WARDROBE:

✒ **THE COMBO PLATTER:** Most likely, the individual color lipsticks you buy are complementary. Wearing one, two, three, even four or five colors together can create really great results. If you normally wear just one of your lipsticks at a time, try adding others on top. Most likely you will find new colors and shades that are even more fabulous than the individual ones. You can also buy a small artist's palette and mix your colors there. Many makeup artists break up the lipsticks they buy, and crush the pieces into the palette.

LIPSTICK RECYCLE-OLOGY: When you run low on a lipstick, scoop it all out from the tube and put it in a little plastic pot. My friend Angela suggested this idea. Often she will put a number of different lipsticks in there together, which she blends and thereby creates new colors. She figures all the colors she likes look good one at a time on her lips, so they must work well when they're mushed together. If you run low on the lipstick in a tube, you can scoop out what is left, add a little Vaseline, put it in a pot, heat over a light flame, stir, and your color is recycled into a new, perhaps more sheer lipstick.

IF YOUR LIPSTICK IS DISCONTINUED: There are a few companies that will recreate a lipstick for you, including the company Three Custom Color Specialists, located in New York. They blend shades to specifications if you send them what's left in the vial.

"As the lips are a nucleus of nerves and surrounded by very many muscles, their contour is changed with every passing thought, and, of all the features, they are the most susceptible of action and the most direct indicators of feelings."

— TURN-OF-THE-CENTURY BEAUTY MANUAL

"If eyes are windows of the soul, lips are the mirror of our mood."

— BOBBI BROWN[11]

"The great thing about lipstick is that it is the one product that can totally change your mood and lift your spirits. It can make you feel playful and even naughty."

— FACE STOCKHOLM'S MARTINA ARFWIDSON

FINDING THE RIGHT COLOR:

In *The World's Best-kept Beauty Secrets,* **Diane Irons** writes: "Take a coral lipstick and a pink lipstick. If your skin more closely resembles the pink, you have pink undertones. The closer match to the coral means that you have 'yellow' undertones."

- **Olive and brown skin** tones work well with cinnamon colors.

- **Bobbi Brown suggests brown-based lipsticks** as being the most natural compliment to most complexions.

- **Colors shouldn't be your enemy:** Cristina Carlino of Philosophy Cosmetics recommends "never wearing colors that make the teeth look yellow. Don't wear a color just because it's in fashion if it does something detrimental to your personal look."

- **If yellow teeth are a problem,** pinks, plums, and mauves will make them look whiter. Avoid browns and corals, which make it worse.

- **If your color changes on you:** Use a gold-toned lipcolor under the shade you usually wear. Powder also helps to create a barrier against your body chemistry (which is often the culprit for curdling colors). To see if a color turns on you, test it on the back of your hand and walk around the store for ten minutes—it often will change during that time.

"The current lipstick trend I see is the freedom of color. It is my favorite trend. There is not only one color of the day like the pale pastels and frosts of the sixties and the red of the fifties, now it is about the mood of the moment. What you are feeling is what you will wear."

— FRANÇOIS NARS

"Red lipstick is the most flattering thing a woman has on. You don't need anything else. Just a great pair of red lips and some black mascara and you're out the door."

—ACTRESS PERI GILPIN[12]

TAKING CONTROL OF YOUR COLORS:

- **LIGHTENING AND DARKENING:** It's as easy as finger paint! A dark or bright shade can be lightened with a lighter color; you can pump up a paler shade by mixing in a dark color. You can mix and blend until you get the desired hue and intensity.

- **NIGHT AND DAY:** Estèe Lauder: "If you apply the darker color over the lighter in the evening hours, you'll have the most exquisite mouth in the world. In the daylight be sure to blend the lighter color over the deeper one. . . . Two colors give a rich, textured vibrancy that's simply magnificent." (from *Estèe: A Success Story*)

- **DARK COLORS—TO MAKE A VAMPIRE COLOR LESS EXTREME AND SEVERE:** Kevyn Aucoin advises toning down the severity of a very dark lipstick by putting a taupe or brownish-gray pencil around it. Also, if you apply the color from the middle of the lip out, concentrating on the center of the mouth, you can keep the corners softer and the whole look more subtle.[13]

SOME COLOR RECIPES

🖌 **WAY BANDY'S HONEY DOT MIX:** Bandy suggests making a pale honey-golden lipcolor by placing the following dots on the hand and mixing them all together with a brush: one dot of gold powder eyeshadow, two drops of a beige liquid foundation, and three dots of clear lip gloss.

🖌 **WAY BANDY'S PURPLISH DOT MIX:** Another Bandy dot recipe: Mix "one dot of chalk-white cover stick, two dots of violet powder eyeshadow, two dots of rose-pink cream rouge, and three dots of clear lip gloss." Mixed together, you have a fuchsia-orchid lipcolor.

TEXTURE, PLAY AND EXPERIMENTATION

"Makeup is very much like music, when each note fits into a chord to create its own unique sound. Each face has within, its own chords and harmonies. Each color, each texture . . . must come together to allow one's face to sing its melody. Like a symphony, makeup tells a story, evokes your emotions, draws you in or pushes you away. It can be dark, light, angelic, or devilish."

— MAKEUP ARTIST MATTHEW
VAN LEEUWIN

"Inspiration comes from studying the face. By observing the features and making discoveries, hints and ideas arise. It is the idea which creates the artist's originality. . . . Makeup is not just technique. Makeup [is] by discovery."

—SHU UEMURA, MAKEUP ARTIST AND CREATOR OF SHU UEMURA COSMETICS

THE SHU UEMURA APPROACH TO CRE-ATING YOUR OWN COLORS: Laura Lee, spokesperson for Shu Uemura, recommends using *texture* alone to vary a color. Color, says Laura, is about how you apply it. You can always make any color work, depending on how it is applied, in what textures, and in what density. Use colors like art supplies to create different effects and textures.

TEXTURES: WORKING WITH MATTES, CREAMS, OPALESCENTS, ETC.: Lip balm under lipstick gives the color a more sheer look. Powdered blush placed on top of a lipstick gives an even more matte look. To make a look softer, blend some moisturizer into your lipstick.

MAKING THE MOST OF YOUR 99 CENTS: Less expensive lipsticks often have a lower price-tag because they don't include as many lubricating ingredients. A little gloss or a sheer light lipstick applied on top of or below the 99¢ Special will keep it from dryness.

SEXING UP A LOOK: Put lip gloss on over your lipstick. The heavier the gloss, the sexier the look. According to my friend Michael, "When there's that high gloss thing, that's like *in-heat lipstick.* The higher the sheen, the more you're looking for action. It's a lure. It focuses the person walking by immediately right on their mouth. By the way, sometimes lipstick can be counterproductive. One hint of overapplication, and we're on to you."

THE PICASSO GUIDE TO LIPSTICK:

"Art is the lie that enables us to realize the truth."
— PABLO PICASSO[14]

Knowing some general art-student color theory will help you when creating different looks with color:

1. **Color balancing:** The eyeshadows and powders used above and around your lipstick color will affect the overall look. Dark tones tend to be intensified when used next to lighter colors (a dark mouth will be even darker when the eye shadow is pale). Brights will appear stronger placed next to neutrals (rich, intense eye shadow will take attention away from a pale mouth).

2. **The Medium:** Color is affected by the medium you use. In painting, the use of watercolor, magic marker, or oil will create a difference in intensity, shade, and hue. The same is true with lipsticks, whether you use a more matte stick (compare to oil paint), a sheer (compare to watercolor), or a drawing pencil or pen (compare to pencils and crayons).

ALL YOU NEED IS LIPSTICK—IT'S MORE THAN A ONE-TRICK PONY:

> "Lipstick and mascara are the two most important cosmetic tools; the two that women can't do without. If you have only a few minutes—lipstick is the thing to use—within just those few minutes, lipstick gives vivacity to the face."
>
> —DIEGO DALLA PALMA

I don't think Diego meant this—but it is true that lipstick can do a number of makeup jobs beyond the standard lips-only route. One recent example of lipstick as a one-trick pony was Kevyn Aucoin's use of a single shade of Yves Saint Laurent Ice Gold lipstick for an Isaac Mizrahi show, as eye shadow, blush, and on the lips themselves, creating an appealing monochromatic look.

EYE MAKEUP IN DRAG AS LIPSTICK, AND OTHER EXCUSES TO MAKE EVERYTHING YOU TOUCH A LIPSTICK:

You can let your lipstick impersonate eye shadow, blush, and more.

- **LIPSTICK ON THE EYEBROWS:** Lipstick, especially a clear gloss, will hold your eyebrows in a particular shape or arch, and adds a glisten. A little gold-colored lipstick drawn in also creates a very nice effect.

- **LIPSTICK AS A HAIR MASCARA:** You can use wild lipcolors like pink and orange in your hair for dramatic streaks, or, for another hair need, avoid harsh dyes and use a black lipstick to cover gray.

🖌️ **LIPSTICK AS AN EYESHADOW:** Anything from a gold to a brown, a clear shimmer to pinks and violets, and even reds make for a great look. It is best to use them as highlighter over your *eye socket,* not on the lid, as lipsticks can sometimes irritate the eyes, and lipliners should not be used on the eye area at all.

🖌️ **LIPSTICK AS A BLUSH:** Neutral-colored lip pencils can be used for contouring, sculpting, and shading the face (the sides of the nose, cheek bones, jaw, etc.).

🖌️ **OR TRY JOAN COLLINS' ADVICE:** "If you run out of lip gloss use Vaseline . . . and if you run out of blusher, blend your lipstick in the palm of your hand with a little cold cream." (From *Health Youth and Happiness: My Secrets.*)

🖌️ **LIPS AND NIPPLES, NIPPLES AND LIPS:** Guerlain's Creme de la Forte, originally marketed as a nipple cream for nursing mothers (the nipple is same type of skin as the mouth) has become a best-selling lip product in Europe.

🖌️ **A WARNING ON REVERSE SWITCHING:** Many cosmetic guides suggest using eyeliner on the lips, or eyeshadows, powders, or foundation creams. This should be done with extreme caution. If you use any of these products on your lips, remember, you will most likely be ingested them. The ingredients should be safe if ingested, and most often products for the eyes or face are not formulated with this precaution taken into account.

GROWING OLD WITH LIPSTICK:

"One's eyes are what one is; one's mouth is what one becomes."

— JOHN GALSWORTHY

AS WE GET OLDER, lips tend to lose color, so lipstick becomes a way to replace that lost color. Upper lips especially tend to get thinner. Lipstick can *soften them up*. Mauve works well. Stay away from oranges, which bring out the increasing yellowness in teeth. Pink corals are good for lighter skin tones. If you are used to wearing a particular dark color, and then notice it is too harsh as you age, add a lightener on top of it, or some kind of shimmer.

FIT AND HEALTHY LIPS, THE MEDICINE CABINET, AND LIPSTICK GYMNASTICS:

1) KEEP LIPS HEALTHY:

The skin of your lips is extremely thin and contains no oil glands, so it can dry out easily. If you're prone to dryness, wear a protective balm when you sleep. Honey is also good. During the day, avoid matte lipsticks. When lips chap or obtain cold sores, avoid spicy foods and drink lots of water. Cracked lips may also be a sign of problems in the lower digestive tract. Check this possibility with a doctor.

2) SEND YOUR MOUTH TO THE GYM:

✔ **BEFORE YOU BEGIN THE EXERCISE PROCESS, ASSESS YOUR MOUTH:** "All the beauty products in the world can't disguise a disagreeable expression," writes Eternal Lipstick Ambassador Joan Crawford. "Have you ever noticed that when you say 'no' you begin to resemble a prune-faced schoolmarm? . . . There are more than thirty facial muscles we use for different expressions, and it's a good idea to pamper the important ones. Facial muscles can sag quickly, but there are some easy ways of keeping them toned up. . . . Open your mouth as wide as you can and at the same time purse your lips as if you're trying to whistle. Hold it for ten seconds. . . . Put your thumb and forefinger inside your mouth and try to push your fingers out—at the same time forcing your cheeks in. Hold for another count of ten. For heaven's sake be sure you're alone when you do these, because you'll look ridiculous."

✔ **ANOTHER TAKE ON MOUTH ASSESSMENT:** "Looking at your face in the glass, all unadorned, let's try a few experiments. Laugh heartily. How did that look? Did you find you drew your lips too far back and showed your gums? Now try a few sentences aloud. Have you any queer mannerisms of twisting your lips when you talk? Is it compressed and puckered? Are the corners down? Most people's mouths look their best when the slightest smile hovers at the corners. Does yours? After a few experiments you will discover quite a lot about your mouth that will be useful to remember when the glass is not there. May we have the lipstick now, please?" (From *The Natural Way to Beauty,* 1946.)

3) EXERCISE THE MOUTH:

🖌 **KEEPING LIPS LIMBER—LIP AEROBICS AND OTHER WAYS TO KEEP THE LIPS LOOKING BEST FOR LIPSTICK:** To keep the mouth in a flexible, unclamped position, say A-E-I-O-U several times over, exaggerating each letter. Or, as a 1930s beauty manual instructs: "Place strips of tape at the corners of your mouth as you do housework. This will remind you not to frown and thereby destroy your sweet expression. No brand of lipstick can fix a scowl. So keep the lines in your lips up up up!"

FINAL TOUCHES: THE BREATH AND TEETH BEHIND THE LIPSTICK:

🖌 The last thing you need to go with your lipstick is bad breath. Fresh spearmint leaves, parsley, fennel and cardamon seeds are good for healthy breath. Also, breathing through the nose rather than the mouth does not dry out saliva as much, which also may effect gum health and breath. To brighten and whiten your teeth, brush with a toothpaste that contains bicarbonate of soda.

LIPSTICK ETIQUETTE:

Most etiquette books include a commentary on lipstick. And most etiquette scribes agree: applying lipstick in public is allowed (applying other makeup is not). There are some other subcategories of lipstick etiquette as well, including rules for the very private life of lipstick. Here are some hints, perhaps a little extreme, on the subject of lipstick etiquette in the privacy of the bedroom, from two lipstick authorities of the past.

> **ADVICE FROM OVID, CIRCA 20 B.C.:** "Don't let your love find the boxes displayed on your dresser. . . . Hide the tricks of your beautifying arts. Your artifice should go unsuspected. Keep in seclusion while in the midst of your beautifying activities, for though such actions may serve well, it is not pleasing to watch their application. . . . On no account let your lover come upon you surrounded by the accoutrements of your cosmetic art. Who could help but feel disgust at the thick paint on your face melting and running down onto your breasts?" (i.e.—go easy, and hide the evidence).[15]

This was perhaps more thoroughly explained about 1,981 years later.

> **ADVICE FROM THE COSMO GIRL'S GUIDE TO THE NEW ETIQUETTE, CIRCA 1961 A.D.:** "Decide which are your 'survival' cosmetics. . . . These are to become your essentials. You must wear these 24 hours a day, 365 days a years, until you are too old to care. I have not been seen without my essentials for three years, and yet I lead an active, almost normal life. . . .

More makeup disappears [in bed] than anywhere else. And the bed is where you need it most! Every girl having an affair should have a magnifying mirror and her essentials makeup kit hidden under the bed. While her lover sleeps, she can make repairs. Note: Always wake up before he does. You will have to survey the damage. . . . Show him your yearly budget. Under makeup, write the figure $3.50 and add hopefully in the margin—'If the price of blush-pink lipstick doesn't go up!' Build a secret compartment in your purse. In the open part, display a neat little comb and a compact and a new tube of Chap Stick."[16]

CHAPTER EIGHT

LIPSTICK LABORATORY

Suburban Witchcraft at Home

or

The Mad Scientist's Lipstick

LIPSTICK RECIPES TO MAKE AT HOME:

Well-formed, shiny lip *sticks* like the ones we buy are actually quite difficult to make at home, since the process relies so much on creating controlled, exact temperatures. Balms and glosses, however, are relatively easy. For recipes that call for beeswax, you can use candles bought at a religious supply store, but make sure it is labelled *pure* beeswax. Most other ingredients can be bought at health food stores and herb shops, natural body product shops, and aromatherapy supply stores. Beeswax usually comes in little cakes or bricks.

Max Factor spent hours experimenting in his lab, as did Helena Rubinstein. Stila Cosmetics' Jeanine Lobell

169

made lipsticks at home with her microwave. Brooke Hargrove of Uni Cosmetics had her very own lipstick-making machine in her New York brownstone. Carol Shaw created lipsticks at home for celebrity clients, which she would bring with her to their makeup sessions.

So put on your couture suit, high heel pumps, pearls, gold earrings, and red lipstick and, like Helena Rubinstein, you too can be a domestic mad scientist in the kitchen.

WORKING WITH INGREDIENTS TO MAKE YOUR MIXTURES HARDER OR SOFTER

Lip balms usually consist of one part beeswax to two and a half parts oil.

As you create your lipsticks, add more beeswax for a harder consistency, as desired.

To make softer, glosslike lipsticks, adjust your ingredients to one part (or one ounce) of beeswax to three parts (or three ounces) of oil.

It is always important that you use oven-safe containers when heating mixtures on a stovetop, or in a microwave. Tin pots, aluminum, and iron will react to the ingredients. You should always use non-reactive pots, such as enamel-coated ones.

THE MOST SIMPLE RECIPES:

EASY BEESWAX LIP BALM

2 tablespoons—beeswax, grated

½ tablespoon—coconut oil

Use this recipe as a first test, to see how to work with the elementary stage of mixing and heating. Grate beeswax, then mix with the coconut oil, and place in a microwave, heating briefly (heat for one minute, then test consistency). You may want to put it in for another minute. By trying it at twenty seconds, half a minute, one minute, or two minutes, you will get a sense of the different possible consistencies.

Stir well, then put into a container and let cool.

VERY BERRY LIP GLOSS

One cup of berries (cranberry, blueberry, raspberry, blackberry)

Aloe vera gel or petroleum oil, to be measured by liquid dropper

Smash berries into a fine paste, measuring one teaspoon at a time. If using a berry with seeds, put through cheesecloth or a fine sieve.

Add drops of aloe vera gel or Vaseline, adding more berries, more gel, or more oil until you have the desired texture and consistency.

Mix different-colored berries as you wish for desired color. If you'd like, you can add drops of food coloring to alter the colors further.

INTERMEDIATE LEVEL:

BASIC NEUTRAL LIPSTICK

1/4 cup—grated beeswax

3 tablespoons—vegetable shortening

1 tablespoon—almond oil

2 tablespoons—cocoa butter

Mix all ingredients together in an ovenproof container. This will seem almost like a dessert batter as you mix it.

Heat in microwave for 1–2 minutes on high, until it is completely melted into a pale gold liquid.

Pour into a small and shallow greased pan lined with foil. The best size is about 5" × 3", if you don't have a pan that size, try a lined box.

Let cool. Once the mixture is slightly hardened, you can cut it with a knife into separate sticks of lipstick. You can then roll the sticks into cigarlike shapes, and place in clean lipstick tubes.

HEALING LIPSTICKS:

CASTOR OIL AND LANOLIN LIP BALM FOR DRY LIPS

1 teaspoon—grated beeswax

1 teaspoon—castor oil

1 teaspoon—lanolin

Using the water-bath technique of heating, put the ingredients in a glass measuring cup, and then heat in a pan of boiling water. Use a medium heat.

Once melted, pour the mixture into tiny jars, like miniature jam jars.

Let cool completely (approximately twenty minutes).

When you use this lip balm, you'll find that the lanolin and castor oil will quickly soothe dry lips.

LIP BALM WITH ALMOND OIL, VITAMINS, AND CANDY

1 teaspoon—cocoa butter

1 teaspoon—beeswax

1 tablespoon—sweet almond oil

1 drop—candy flavoring

3 drops—vitamin E oil

1 teaspoon—paraffin wax

1 teaspoon—petroleum jelly

1 old thoroughly cleaned lipstick tube

Melt ingredients separately.

Pour each ingredient into its own container.

Then, combine them all in a double boiler. Heat and stir.

Once it is well blended, pour the mixture into cleaned-out lipstick vials that are coated with just a little bit of almond oil.

Leave them alone for about one and a half hours, then put them in the fridge.

Once they have hardened nicely, you can further shape them into lipstick bullets in the vial. If you want, decorate your vials with designs (but that's another project!).

MAKING LIP GLOSS FROM CRAYONS:

3—nontoxic crayons

1—pure beeswax candle (one inch in diameter)

3 tablespoons—mineral oil

Take a half-inch slice of your candle and put it in a small heat-resistant cup with the mineral oil.

Then get out your Crayola crayons, or whatever kind you use (just be sure it's nontoxic). Choose the colors you like. Peel off the paper. Put them in a plastic baggie, then smash away at it with a hammer. Next, add the crayons to your heat-resistant cup.

Set your cup in a small saucepan. Just be sure the pan can hold enough water to reach a level of one and a half inches up the side of your cup.

Gently heat.

Stir occasionally (until waxes are melted and color is evenly distributed).

Allow to cool for about 15 minutes

You can try as many times as you'd like with different colored crayons.

FLAVORED LIPSTICKS:

HEAVENLY CHOCOLATE GLOSS

1$\frac{1}{2}$ teaspoons—grated cocoa butter

$\frac{1}{2}$ teaspoon—vitamin E oil

$\frac{1}{2}$ teaspoon—coconut oil

$\frac{1}{4}$ teaspoon—grated chocolate (or three small chocolate chips, either milk or dark chocolate)

Carefully heat cocoa butter, coconut oil, and the vitamin E oil in a microwave.

Slowly stir in chocolate and continue melting.

Continue to stir the mixture from time to time until it's very well blended, returning it to the microwave as needed.

Pour into a cleaned-out plastic box from a candy store or a pillbox. Allow to cool.

With both this recipe and the vanilla gloss, you may notice it smells like some expensive brand lipsticks.

VANILLA GLOSS WITH VITAMIN E

1 tablespoon—grated beeswax

½ tablespoon—grated coconut oil

⅛ teaspoon—vitamin E oil

⅛ teaspoon—vanilla extract

(Note: this makes a very fragrant gloss.)

Take out the beeswax, coconut oil, and vitamin E oil. Pour them together into an ovenproof container. Using a microwave, gently heat your mixture until the beeswax and the two oils are evenly mixed together. Next, stir in the vanilla extract.

Once you have a uniform mixture, pour it into a small lip gloss pot, or again, you can use a little plastic candy box from a candy store.

Set it aside until it cools completely . . . then put on the cap, and it's ready to go. And remember—vanilla is good for calming the nerves!

COLORED LIPSTICKS:

SUNSHINE-SAFFLOWER LIPSTICK

Take a handful of safflower flowers (scarlet-orange-yellow in color), and soak in two cups of boiling water. Let cool. To this liquid add three parts rice powder and one part kaolin until you have a smooth paste. Use as a lipstick or rouge.

ROSE LIP GLOSS

2 tablespoons—beeswax

¼ cup—almond oil

1 drop—oil of rose

⅛ teaspoon—carmine

Melt wax over a low heat.

Stir in carmine. Go easy with the pigment, adding carmine in slowly. You may want to control the intensity of the color.

Slowly add almond oil and the oil of rose. Mix slowly, and enjoy the aroma.

Let sit until cooled. Store in clear pots or gloss containers.

PURPLE-PINKISH-RED LIPCOLOR

1 tablespoon—grated beeswax

2 tablespoons—almond oil

⅛ to 1 teaspoon—beet juice or beet root powder (purple-red in color)

Mix oil and wax together. Heat in microwave on high for 1–2 minutes.

Add beet juice or powder. Stir.

Even though the mix may separate during the process, it will stay together when it cools down.

Add more juice or powder for desired color, once the mixture, which can be anywhere from pink to purple to red, begins to cool. Play and experiment with the coloring.

Fill cleaned-out gloss pots with your potion.

RED ROSE SEMI-SHEER STAIN

4 ounces—almond oil

¼ ounce—beeswax

1 teaspoon—alkanet root

2–3 drops of rose oil

(Note: This recipe will take you several days.)

Day 1: Mix alkanet root and almond oil together in a jar.

Day 2–10: Stir your mix once a day. Keep it at room temperature.

Day 10: Strain the oil. Melt the beeswax in a pan. Slowly add in the strained oil. Use a wooden spoon to mix your concoction. Once it is even in consistency and color, let it cool.

Then, add drops of rose oil.

Not only does this lipstain have a lovely color, it smells good, too.

Once you hit an advanced level of lipstick-making, you can also make different formats of lipstick. With some practice, you can roll some paper around your lip crayons and make it look just like a Crayola. You can make matchstick lipsticks by placing the end of a Q-tip in the mixture and letting it dry on the swab. And finally, for the most advanced and adventurous, you can fool around with the consistencies of your lipstick potions, and go as far as making lipstick modeling clay.

LIPSTICK YOU CAN EAT
OR Julia Child's Lipstick

You'd be surprised how many people confess to eating lipstick when they were kids.

But then, who wouldn't? It's colorful. It smells good. It looks like candy.

But what about those of us who eat it sort of by accident, by just wearing it? It's reported that we eat about fifty percent of the lipstick we wear, and the average American woman eats 1–3 tubes of lipstick a year, depending on her level of lipstick addiction (women lower on the addiction spectrum tend toward one tube). The Food and Drug Administration uses the phrase "incidentally ingested" to describe this kind of chowing down lipstick without actually meaning to.

It's precisely this fact that has gotten the attention of both chemists and advertisers, in hopes of creating a lipstick that can be advertised as something you can eat.

But wouldn't it be nice if you really could eat lipstick, *really* chow down? Instead of eating a pint of Häagen-Dazs, how about if you could scarf down a couple of tubes without worry?

For those of you who might crave the taste of a thick and shiny lippy chunk of vibrant red, here's a few recipes for lipsticks you really can eat.

ULTRAVIOLET POP BEET LIPSTICK

In the 1960s, Warhol superstar Ultra Violet may have single-handedly increased the sale of beets in New York when word spread that she painted beet juice on her lips to give her that ultraviolet glow. But any inflated beet sales didn't continue for long. After all, Eau de Beets has never sustained a following. Years later, Ultra Violet revealed her secret beet beauty trick in her memoir, *Famous for 15 Minutes: My Years with Andy Warhol*:

"Using fresh beets on my cheeks and lips, I achieve an alive transparent tint. To renew my lipcolor during an evening I pull out of my gold mesh evening purse a gigantic fresh beet with the green leaves still dangling on their red stems. With a tiny gold knife I slice a morsel from the beet and rub it on my lips and cheeks in full view of the staring onlookers. The shade it imparts is neither red nor pink nor orange but an out-of-this-world rouge-violet." Bonus tip: "When there is a long wait between meals, I head off starvation by nibbling a few mouthfuls of the white rice powder that I dust on my face from a beautiful cloisonne compact."

SLEEK BERRY-HONEY POT-O-GLOSS

1 tablespoon—almond oil

10—fresh blueberries, blackberries, or cranberries

1 teaspoon—honey

Mix oil, honey, and berries together. Put in microwave for 1–2 minutes. Stir completely; gently mash berries. Let sit 5 minutes. Strain through a fine sieve so all bits of berry and seed are gone. Stir; let cool completely. Spoon into a recycled gloss pot container.

CANDY STAIN LIPSTICKS

This recipe was created by a group of second-graders at a New Jersey public school, as a science experiment. It may not have the super-promised magic of all-day staying power, but it does taste and smell good.

Gun Nowak, cofounder of FACE Stockholm Cosmetics, revealed in a *People* magazine interview that since she was not allowed to wear lipstick as a girl, she resorted to what must be the same exact recipe.

Take red hard candy, such as a red lollipop. Rub on your lips for about ten minutes. That's it!

If you'd then like to glamourize the look with a frosty glow:

Get some sugar, mix it with water, and apply little dabs on top.

To change colors, follow the red lollipop with a purple, orange, or brown lollipop.

It's not the most exotic of recipes, but it works.

CHAPTER NINE

THE TIME TRAVELER'S LIPSTICK

Making Lipstick from Different Periods in History Featuring Recipes, Advice, and Techniques from Lipstick Superstars of the Past

"If we were perpetuating the gestures of the twentieth century for posterity, putting on lipstick would head the list."

— *Vogue* MAGAZINE, 1933

ORANGE SCARAB EGYPTIAN TANGEE: Get a stick from outside. Attach a soft feathered material to its end to make it into a long brush. Now get the carmine (the ancient Egyptian doesn't know this, but this is the same material that will be used for about the next 5,000 years in lipstick). If you don't feel like using carmine, or don't have any, get some red ocher pigment. Put this in a base of fat or oil. Or you can just mix with a little water. Apply to lips. Be sure to do your eye makeup first, which is much more important. Remember, eye makeup fulfills religious purposes, and is applied with reverence to the god Horus. And you definitely don't want to piss off any gods for the sake of lipstick. If you have a slave around, she will assist you, mixing the powders with her own saliva. She'll also throw some perfume in. Try to get the color in the realm of a reddish brown, magenta, or orange-red. Stay a little to the left of bright red if you can, since most priests will tell you that's the color of evil. You can keep your liprouge in pots or rolled up in leaves.

HOT VENUS BLACKBERRY SHIMMER: To be an ancient Greek superprostitute: First, take a scented liquid, put it in mouth, and roll around with tongue. Once your mouth is ready to go, get out your puperissium (a root from Syria), macerate with vinegar, and apply to lips. Vermillion and poederos (a red root) can also be used for different textures and shimmers. Corn flour or barley meal powdered on the face will accentuate the redness of your lips. If you're not a prostitute, sorry, but you can't wear extravagant makeup. You might as well get used to life as an ancient version of *Father Knows Best.*

RAMBLING ROMAN ROSE: Ovid may have been the Kevyn Aucoin of ancient Rome. The beauty secret section of his celebrated book, *The Art of Love,* was as big a deal in its time as Kevyn's books are in his. Ovid, however, did not suggest blotting, reapplying color, and then using powder for longer-lasting lipstick, but simpler hints, more concerned with social correctness—more along the lines of the "Do's and Don'ts" section at the back of *Glam-*

our magazine. For the few home recipe tips Ovid did offer, he recommended buying fucus, alkanet, and crushed poppy leaves to get a lovely Roman Rosey Glow. Or, you could make a nice wine color with, well, wine.

ROMANTIC ROSE SHEEP FAT MATTE: From the medieval glamour guides, here's a recipe for making lipstick at home: Go outside. Get a root. Dry it. Pulverize it. Add some sheep fat and whiteners to get desired color. If you are upper class, go for a bright pink. If lower class, use a cheaper earth red. If you are having trouble being pale, and have the money to pay for it, get yourself bled. If you're alive during the Crusades, wait for the Crusaders to come back, as they'll bring some glamorous and exotic dyes, ointments, and spices, and you'll be able to experience the makeup golden age of the Middle Ages.

Always be aware of the current hierarchy of sins currently issued by the church (note: it changes according to who is pope), and be sure vanity isn't too close to the top.

If you want to dye your hair to complete your look, stay away from red, the sign of the witch. Bright yellow hair color is usually a big hit. Don't even think of having your lips tattooed, by the way—it's outlawed. The church does not see this as appropriate behavior, what with God watching. Stay away from saints, too—they're busy writing long treatises on the evils of your favorite makeup. Two great writers in this How Dare You School: St. Cyprian and St. Ambrose. If you incited their wrath, it was pretty much all over for you and for your lipstick.

And in place of *Harper's Bazaar* and *Vogue*: One great lipstick sage of the period was Henri de Mondeville, the French king's physician in 1306. Henri realized early on that he could make extra dough and acquire more prestige by giving out makeup tips.

ELIZABETHAN FIRE AND ICE: You can be just like Queen Elizabeth I, who made many of her cosmetics all by herself. But before you do your lipstick—do your hair à la Liz: Take some fat from a freshly killed puppy dog and mix it with apples, then grease it over your hair. Next, mix in a small pan: egg white, powdered egg shells, alum, borax, and white poppy seeds. Spread over forehead to kill wrinkles. Then, after applying powder and rouge, put on lip dye, and cover with a glaze of egg white. You may use the same rouge on your lips that you use for your cheeks. For chapped lips, take some sweat from behind your ears and rub onto mouth.

If you'd like teeth to go with those lips, false teeth made from ivory, silver, mother-of-pearl, and porcelain were plundered from battlefields and slaughterhouses. These could be inserted to give your lips an extra allure. After applying all your makeup, go outside wearing an oval mask with cutouts for eyes; to be held in place with a button grasped between your teeth (whether they're your own teeth or those of a dead animal is not important).

Warning: Be sure to watch the European laws about what could be worn by whom.

A REAL LIVE LIPSTICK, CIRCA 1559: Take some ground alabaster or plaster of Paris. Combine with a coloring ingredient. Mix into a paste, then form into a pencil shape. Place in the sun, let dry and solidify.

CLASS CONSCIOUS RUBY LUSTRE (early 1600s): Keeping up with the rules of color and class, if you are an upper-class babe, who goes for an enameled look, use a moist cherry red. If you're a lower-class wench, the laws suggest you go for a cheaper ocher red. It's best if your lower lip is fuller than the upper. Here is a nice recipe for Spanish fucus from just one of the many recipe books available to you (this one is from *Lady Tail-Bush's Book*):

> Water of gourds, of radish, the white beans,
> Flowers of glass, of thistles, rose marine,
> Raw honey, mustard seed, and bread dough-bak'd,
> The crums o'bread, goats-milk, and white of eggs.
> Camphire, and lily-roots, the fat of swans,
> Marrow of veal, white pigeons, and pine-kernels,
> The seeds of nettles, purseline, and hares-glass;
> Limons, thin-skin's . . .

And it goes on: "The right lustre, but two drops rubb'd on with a piece of scarlet, makes a lady of sixty look as sixteen."

MIDNITE SPANISH GLOW DE BRILLO (France/ England, 1700s): Get some Spanish Rouge (a pad of hair similar to a Brillo pad, with red coloring instead of blue soap inside), which can be used on both cheeks and lips. Put this on before you go to Maria Gunning's funeral, the famous beauty who officially died from "addiction to cosmetics." Spanish Rouge is only one of your options. If you don't get off on the pad approach, you can make your own sixteenth-century lipstick out of ground plaster of Paris, colored to choice. Always try to use the brightest scarlet you can find. In shaping the mouth, go for the tiny bow effect. To fill in the hollow where your teeth have fallen out, push in some plumpers. Don't worry about the plumpers making you lisp. Lisping is fashionable now. You can also use your liprouge to color your fingernails if you feel like it. Throw a couple of patches (beauty marks) around your mouth to state your political affiliation and sexual interests. If you're feeling slutty, definitely be sure to put some patches near the lip. Once again, if you'd like some teeth to go with those lips—you can add a pair transplanted from a healthy young peasant. To take your lipstick off, use a wash ball made of rice powder, flour, starch, white lead, and red roots.

MARIE ANTOINETTE'S "RED-LIPPED HEAD-LESS WONDER": Here's a nice little recipe for "Red Pomatum for the Lips" that Marie might have enjoyed. If not Marie, someone during the eighteenth century certainly had fun with it:

> Take an Ounce of white Wax and of an Ox's Marrow, three Ounces of white Pomatum, and melt all in a Bath-Heat. Add a Dram of Alkanet, and stir the Mass till it acquires a red Color. Others chuse to use the Ointment of Roses, which is thus prepared: Take Hog's Lard wash'd in Rose-Water, red Roses, and pale Roses; beat all in a Mortar, mix them all together, and let them macerate for two Days. Then melt the Lard and strain it, and add the same Quantity of Roses as before. Let them macerate in the Fat for two Days, and afterwards let the Mass boil in a Bath-Head. Strain it with Expression, and keep it for Use. Some are accustom'd to wash their Lips with pure Brandy in order to make them look red." (From *Abdeker: or the Art of Preserving Beauty,* by Antoine Le Camas, 1754.)

ANOTHER RECIPE FROM THE 1700s: "Take Benjamin, Brasil Wood, Roch-Alum, of each half an Ounce. Macerate the Whole in a Pint of strong Brandy for the Space of twelve Days; shake the Bottle every Day, let it be well cork'd, and keep it for Use."

MARTHA WASHINGTON'S LIP SALVE: Martha made pots of lip salve that were put together by carefully mixing wax, hogs' lard, spermaceti, almond oil, balsam, alkanet root, raisins, and sugar, and then handed the recipe down to her children and grandchildren.

"BUTTER APPLAUSE"–STAGE ACTRESS' LIPSTICK, CIRCA 1845: Take a fresh pat of butter, mix with vermilion, work into a paste and apply to lips. Use a rabbit's foot for application. Pure vegetable food coloring can also be painted on.

MAKEUP TRICKS FROM SARAH BERNHARDT: As described by the Divine Sarah in her book, *The Art of the Theatre,* "If the character was a passionate, ill-fated woman . . . I would eliminate the bow of my upper lip in order to produce a straight and inflexible line. My face would then take on a mysterious remoteness. If my character . . . was a victim of circumstance seeking the meaning of life . . . I would shorten the corners of my mouth, the lower lip of which I would paint with cerise . . . my face would [then] amuse me with its sanctimonious naïveté."[1]

LONG-WEARING SCARLET SLUT WITHOUT SPF-15 (for the Victorian Prostitute Look): Rouge your lips in greasepaints of very basic colors, but try to use the brightest red you can find. Don't go to much more trouble than that. Draw a rounded, bow-shaped lip line, and smudge it for extra effect.

LATE NINETEENTH CENTURY OPTIONS: Some discreet products on the shelves included "Tampons au Rouge" (colored crepons that came in ivory handles), and "Rouge en Crepons" (bits of silk or cotton gauze twisted into a plug, filled with color, and some moisturizing alcohol or wine, then rubbed onto lips). But what kind of lips? According to beauty scribe Harriet Hubbard Ayers: "A perfect mouth is of medium size, the upper lip bow-shaped, and under nearly straight. The lips should be neither too thick, which gives them a sensual expression, nor too thin." Beauty books, such as the one written by Harriet, emphasized clean, sweet breath, which was always an indicator of a pure and sincere character. At the end of the Lip Toilet chapter, a few discreet recipes were thrown in, but almost always pretending to be for the care of chapped lips. Such as this one:

> *Peruvian Lip Salve* (considered the most glamorous of all the lip salves):
> 1 oz Spermaceti ointment, 15 grains Balsam of Peru, 15 grains alkanet root, 5 drops of cloves. Digest the alkanet in the ointment at gentle heat, until the latter is a deep rose color, then pass through a coarse strainer. When slightly cooled, stir in the balsam, give a few moments to settle, then pour off the clear portion and add the oil of cloves. You can make this or any other mixture a glycerinated pomade by adding one-sixth or one-eighth part glycerine, and a drop or two of any other essential oil can be added. (From *The Woman Beautiful,* a popular period guide.)

SUPER DISCREET ROSE LIP SALVE (late 1890s): A recipe to make at home when no one is looking: Take equal parts washed lard (melted) and rose leaves. Mix. In two days, remelt the mass, press out the fat, and repeat the process using fresh rose leaves of equal weight. Press and strain. For more red, color with a little alkanet root. This will make the same rose ointments sold in the French pharmacies of the period. Or, if you're a nineteenth-century scaredy-cat, try Plan B instead:

1) Bite lips. 2) Wet some pigmented tissue paper, and pat on lips. 3) Get some squashed berries and put on with fingertips.

1910s DISCRETE ROSEGLOW: Madame Cavalier, a beauty expert of the period, recommends that your lips "should be a deep pink or a light red, at least three shades lighter than the blood." This recipe from a 1910 beauty book, is not recommended for home use. Color could be adjusted to fit Madam's theory:

Take 3 drachms of boric acid, ¼ drachm of carmine, 2 ounces of soft paraffin, 1 ounce of hard paraffin, and otto of rose, sufficient to perfume. Mix together. Discreetly apply to lips.

TO MAKE YOUR OWN 1920s ROSEBUD OR CUPID'S LIPS: In general, spend the day doing exercises on your own to get your lips into the right shape before you put on your lipstick. Do so by saying "prunes and prisms" as much as you can through the day to get a rosebud for a mouth. When putting on your lipstick, use your fingers—two fingers for the top lip, one finger for the bottom. If you're going for a cupid's bow, get out a lip pencil and draw on the bow. To finish up, paint on a false beauty spot.

A 1930s LIPSTICK: The following recipe is from a cosmetic guidebook from the thirties for those in the makeup business. This is to give you an idea of the formula of the period, but is not to be tried at home: Take 2 ounces of paraffin wax; 3 ounces of white Vaseline; 1 ounce of white beeswax; 3 ounces of ceresine; 1 ounce of titanium dioxide; and 6 drachm of carmine. Melt waxes over a water bath. Grind in finely powdered carmine, then mix in titanium dioxide. Strain the hot liquid through linen and set aside. When temperature comes down to 110 degrees F, pour into molds to set.

CHAPTER TEN

GEORGE WASHINGTON CARVER'S LIPSTICK

From the Lost Papers of George Washington Carver: 300 Uses for a Lipstick

Washington Carver had 300 uses for a peanut. This is another version of the Grand Peanut Idea, with some handy, and enlightening uses for a lipstick. Here are the first fifty:

JUVENILE DELINQUENT USES:

1.   If you want to play hookey from school and need to look sick, you'll find that if you put dark eye makeup under your eyes it looks too phony. But lipstick, well

blended and rubbed around the eyes is much more effective.

2.   If you are forced to eat cranberries at Thanksgiving, or some other food that grosses you out, go into the bathroom, rub cranberry-red lipstick around mouth, blot, and repeat. (Or use lipstick colored appropriately to the given food.) Return to table with toilet paper. Put yucky food in the tissue when no one is looking. Draw attention to your lips and say something phony about how delicious the cranberries were.

3.   To feign exhaustion and get out of gym class: Rub and blend lipstick into face. Then, smear on a particularly oil-rich moisturizer to get your face sweating. If done right, this is a highly effective technique for fake exhaustion.

4.   To get even: Put lipstick on your lips. Gently press your lips onto the collar of a person you're pissed off at when they aren't looking. Smear the print a little so that your lip print is not readable as yours. Watch trouble bloom like a flower.

5.   With red lipstick, write nasty things on a mirror. Use a color that matches your message. Proven to be highly therapeutic.

AMATEUR CRIMINAL USES:

6.   Pass messages or contraband materials in a shelled-out lipstick vial to the secret agent you are meeting at the bus station or park bench.

7.   At the prison, in place of the now-defunct iron file in a cake, use the lipstick. Directions: Go to the prison. Pretend you are there to cheer up person you are visiting with a lipstick. Actually, you will have inserted

the standard prisoner's escape file inside the shelled-out lipstick tube. Give them a couple weeks to file down bars, then meet them down by the river.

STICKY SITUATION USES:

8.   To put an end to dating someone you don't know how to say no to: Apply strange orange lipstick. Get it outside of lipline. Smile and giggle after you apply, to show you think you look lovely.

9.   For emergency plumbing uses at home: Take a chunk of the wax to clog up a leak until plumbing services can be obtained.

10.   Use a chunk of the wax to fill in a hole in the wall. Try to match lipstick color to wall paint as best as you can.

USES FOR VERY, VERY NICE PEOPLE (OR IF YOU AREN'T THAT, THEN HERE'S SOME USES FOR BEING A VERY FABULOUS PHONY):

11.   Give a lipstick as a gift. Psychiatrists report that lipstick given to someone who is suffering from depression is a highly effective tool in healing.

12.   If someone's crying in a public bathroom: First, help them wash their face. Then say: "Here, honey, let me put a little lipstick on you." Do it. Instant saintdom. Guaranteed.

MORE WAYS TO WIN FRIENDS AND INFLUENCE PEOPLE VIA LIPSTICK, OR, GAINING SAINTDOM THROUGH LIPSTICK:

13.   Tell someone that you love their lipstick. It's the easiest way to give a compliment and make someone feel

great without getting *too* personal—yet being just personal enough for impact.

MEDICINAL PURPOSE—PSYCHOLOGICAL:

14.   Place in your jacket or pants pocket. Use as a worry bead.

MEDICINAL PURPOSE—PHYSICAL:

15.   Use cleaned-out container as a vial to hold emergency medicine.

CHILD PACIFYING USES:

16.   If you are playing with screaming children who need to be quieted down: Take out a lipstick. Start drawing it on your lips. Then, go beyond the corners of your lips. Then, up the sides of your mouth. Across your nose. Over to your ears. Down neck. Etcetera. This has been scientifically tested on two-, three-, and four-year-olds, who all gave a similar review: "Absolutely Hysterical." They've since asked to play Lipstick Face often.

17.   Empty lipstick vials can be used to roll across floor for "Lipstick Races."

18.   Empty vials can also be used to build structures, if glued together, similar to the high rises made with building blocks.

HALLOWEENOLOGY:

19.   Besides the usual vampire look and fake blood, you can paint on pink or purple sheer/glossy lipsticks to simulate burns. Lip liner that is drawn on the skin and then wiped off, leaves a very convincing scar. These techniques can also be used under the section for Juvenile Delinquent Uses, especially if you need to pretend you were in a knife fight.

20.   Full body lipstick can be used if you'd like to go trick-or-treating as a lipstick.

21.   Make a headdress of lipsticks and go trick-or-treating as an Indian. To make this headdress, paste lipstick onto a bendable piece of cardboard. Attach to your head by a string stapled on to each side of the cardboard strip.

BUSINESS USES:

22.   If you are opening a business and need to differentiate between male and female bathrooms, change the standard man in pants and woman in dress logos to Men = a regular mouth, and Women = a mouth with lipstick.

ARTY FARTY USES:

23.   To make stained glass, take old lipsticks and smear on pieces of glass.

24.   As a medium for performance art piece: 1) Cover yourself with lipstick. 2) Roll around on ground, squealing. 3) Contort body. 4) Stand and bow for applause.

25.   Use lipsticks in place of crayons in a coloring book or in place of colored pencils or watercolor for paint-by-number art.

26.   Melted lipsticks can be used for splatter-design art.

MAKE YOUR OWN LIPSTICK TOTEM OR LIPSTICK MONSTER:

27.   At a toy store, buy yourself a cheap little toy truck or tractor. The cheaper and more breakable the better. Take off the wheels. Paste to the bottom of your lip-

stick. Or, you can buy a wind-up toy—the kind with just feet, no head. Place lipstick on top of it. Wind it up. Watch as everyone runs in terror.

AS A GLAMOROUS FRENCH PERFUME SUBSTITUTE:

28.   Draw lipstick on wrist, then wipe off. Draw on again. Repeat. The color will mostly vanish, but the scent will linger on, and you will be wearing Eau de Lipstick, to bewitch all in sight.

29.   Blend various lipsticks of different scents together in a pot, and create your very own new lipstick perfumes!

MAKING THE MOST OF A VIAL:

30.   Use empty vial as a candleholder for a very small candle or to hold birthday candles on a cake when birthday person has aversion to wax melted on frosting.

31.   Use vials to hold little tiny flowers. Fill with water, and display in a row if you'd like.

32.   Use vial as a shot glass.

33.   Use vials to hold Q-Tips or bobby pins.

34.   Make a chess set after you've collected enough differently shaped vials.

LIPSTICK IN THE KITCHEN:

35.   Make lipstick popsicles. Collect clean, large size lipstick vials. Fill with juice. Place toothpick in middle. Freeze. When it's all done, pull out the tiny popsicle by holding on to the toothpick. Hope for the best.

36.   Make chocolate candies in the shape of lipstick bullets: Insert melted chocolate into cleaned out

vials. Give as gift, especially on Valentine's Day. If you're no good at making candy, you can buy chocolate bars and melt them.

LIPSTICK ART WITH KIDS:

37.   Make lip art prints: Draw liner on just part of your upper lip, then blot on a piece of paper—it will make a nice flying bird. When different people do their lips and add them to the paper, you have many different shapes and sizes of birds flying over a horizon. Make different objects and animals. Some of the ones you can try: A single lip as a worm or a series of mountains with the top lip repeated over and over.

38.   Use empty vial for a doll house. For example, a vial can be the doll house garbage can or laundry basket. You can also paste Velcro on the sides of the lipstick vials and put them together to create a bunch of logs for a fireplace.

LIPSTICK MASTERPIECES:

39.   Take a picture of a reproduction of your favorite artwork (textured Modiglianis, Fauves, Impressionists, and Mirós work best). Take a piece of tracing paper and draw the outlines of the masterpiece. Then cover the back of the tracing paper with pencil, and transfer the outlines on your tracing paper on to drawing paper. Then, color in the outline with your lipsticks (you can also go out and buy cheapies just for this purpose), and recreate/reproduce it in the lipstick medium. Also, if you want, you can melt your lipsticks and do a Jackson Pollock.

LIPSTICK ACCESSORIES:

40.   Make a belt to hold lipsticks, in the style of an around-the-waist bullet-belt.

Jessica Pallingston   **197**

41.   Cover your lipstick vial with fake fur. This makes a nice personalized lipstick vial.

LIPSTICK EARRINGS:

42.   Put dot of lipstick on an earlobe (should be a heavy consistency, and is usually best if it is a glittery metallic). Apply glitter to the coloring for more rhinestone shine.

MAKING LIPSTICK MASTERPIECES ON YOUR LIPS:

43.   Paint your lips with swirls, polka dots, and stripes; lip designs that show landscapes, or make use of abstract designs; lips that have Monet's gardens colored on; lips painted as eyes and noses, etc.

MORE USES FOR LIPSTICK PRINTS:

44.   Leopard-print lips: Make a fabric or wrapping paper with a series of lip prints in the brown and gold colors of a leopard print (you'd be surprised how much a leopard print does look like lip prints).

45.   Lipstick-print wrapping paper: Make a series of lipstick prints in various shapes and colors and textures and expressions. Cut into small pieces. Then paste onto new piece of paper in either abstract or nonabstract form. Go over with a thin gloss shine. This can also be used for collage paper for other projects.

MAKE GLOW-IN-THE-DARK LIPSTICK:

46.   Take pieces of glow-in-the-dark paper or cloth, cut to fit mouth, adhere with tape or nontoxic sticky substance. Then glow.

47.   Buy wax lips; paint them with Day-Glo paint.

TO COVER THE GRAY:

48.   Use a black lipstick to discreetly cover your gray hairs, without having to go the route of heavy dyes. Matte brown and black lipsticks are the best choice.

RUBBER STAMP LIPS:
49.   Get a rubber stamp that has a very small design on it. Stick in melted lipstick, apply to mouth. There you have it: little designs on your lips. Or, if you like, make your own lipstick sealing wax stamp.

PAINT A WALL:
50.   For any of us who painted lipstick on the wall as a child and got in big trouble for it, here's your second chance: a wall completely covered with lipstick, whether a monochrome look, a design/patterned look, a combination of mattes and sheers and glosses, whatever—the overall effect can be gorgeous, as well as a highly therapeutic experience.

EE CUMMINGS' LIPSTICK:
LIPSTICK POEMS, AND HAIKU

Now let the lipstick muse sit down on your face.

Did you ever play Mad Libs? Now is your chance to play Mad Lips. Mad Lips, or as it is more gently called, Lipstick Haiku.

You can also create poems or stories with the names of your lipsticks.

You can paint the words with the lipstick colors themselves.

You can use your own list, or, if you'd like, you can use mine.

Here's a collection of names that are taken from my lipstick collection (all 100 percent certified real lipsticks): Taxi Cab, Mermaid, Fiend, Box Office Gold, Dusk, Wine, Wind, Verve, Toast of the Town, 12, Toast of New York, Scarlet, Bergamot, Juniper, Glisten, 365, Pink Passion, Brun Rose, Devil's Claw, Sweet Manna, Sweet Mama, Marooned, Fiesta, Diva Brown, I'm In Love, Sorbet Creme, 10, Mischief, New York, Belle du Jour, Merlot, Poppy Dust, Phantom, Integrity, Pervette, Raisin, Fire Down Below, Sugar and Spice, Rio, Toffee, Nude, Almost Nude, Nevada, Viva Las Vegas, Moonstone, 110, Nicole, Rosie, Rosewood, Rosetto, Mauvelous, Mauve Like Me, Mauve Dream, Mauvie Star, Hungry, Barely Brown, In the Nude, Really Nude, Nude Supreme, Glistening, Red No. 5, Captive, Star Struck, Wuss, Woo, Bambi, Mystery, Aloof, Trans Europe Express, Piaf, Boysenberry, Fig, Wicked, Marcia Marcia Marcia, Film Noir, Instinct, Oyster, Cowboy, Gidget, Invite, Sea Nymph, Sea Foam, Aquarius, Scorpio, Pink Promises, Temptation, Dominatrix, West End, Inspiration, Ambition, Smile, Milk Maid, Malibu, Desert Moon, M, Please, Amour, Anger, Cherries in the Snow, Icon, Odyssey, Kenya, Natural Valli, Innocence, Decadence, Indolence, Heather Mist, Stonehenge, English Toffee, Dr Pepper, Burberry, Dreamy Winter, Ashes of Roses, Desire, Coffee and Cream, Plum Perfection, Haute Couture, Trailer Trash, XOX, Flame, Red to Remember, Be Mine, Indian Tea, Tea, Eggplant, Heartbreak Heather, Black, Bardot, Barbarella, Cafe au lait, Coffee, Creamy, Russian Red, Flirt, Barely There,

Berry Spacey, Lumina, Gloss, Pink Ice, Princess, Teen Queen, Toreador, Stop Light, Red Light, Times Square, Soho, Wine with Everything, Wine Kiss, Wine Stain, Beauty Stain, Satin, Stain, Society Red, Viva Glam, Viva Glam II, Apple, Alive, Sweetie Pie, Smoooch, Tulip, Ice, Very Berry Moonglow, Plum Shine, Parisian Night, Polyester, Mauve, Fabulous Fuchsia, Fur, Amethyst, Cinema Pink, Rosepetal, Sugarplum, Caramel, Chocolate, Haute Couture Pink, Pinkissimo, Pink Pink, Drink of Water, Sea Nymph, Chilled, Champagne, Luv Me!, Congo, Campfire, Chintz Affair, White Wonder, Pale Fire, Wicked, Delicious, Del Rio, Violets, Ebony Heroine, Disco Smoke, Plum Beautiful Luscious, Paris, Envy, Hot Cross Buns, Heartbreak, Halo, Kiss, Kiss Kiss, Kiss Kiss Kiss, Lust, Sincerity, Wisdom, Intuition, Hunter, Jane, Stella, Kate, Vamp, Tramp, Casablanca, Berlin, Roman Holiday, Metal Glamour, Pina Colada, The Dreamer, Hot to Trot, Vixen, Anger, Love Child, Vin, Gash, Cinnamon, Number 17, Violets, Skitzo, Pearl, Rouge Diabolique, Steamy, Sheer Ambrosia, Milan, Shell, Cabaret, Venus, Mercury, Basic Yellow, Amber, Cinder, King Kong, But Officer, Number 12, Flame, Bloody Mary, Soul Kiss, Wet Thunder, Since I Met You, Come, Phantom, Nevada, Dublin, Meditation in Purple, Misunderstood, Aloha, Xanadu, Plague, Sun, Chili Pepper, Port, Hot Mustard, Hot Hot Hot, Shocked, Reckless, Diva, Jupiter, Just Looking, Electric Orchid, Electric Banana, Skin, Twig, Hell's Bells, Flaunt, Cauldron Smoke, Vampire Red, Carnaby Street, Honeypie, Double Fudge, Splurge, Extravagant, Purple Haze, Roach, Frill, Cobweb, Poison Ivy, Tree Frog, Bloody Maria, Blood, Blood and Wine, Jezebel, Slippery When Wet, Fender Bender, Tailgate, Side Swipe, Zsa Zsa, Cadaver, Bond Girl, Dietetic Hunger, Divine Flesh, Flesh Light, Porneia, Deadly Nightshade, Poodle, Whoopee!, Surrender Dorothy.

Some of the lipstick poems and haiku I created from the names of my lipsticks:

Gash/Sugarplum/Amber/Stain/Satin/Gloss/Pink Ice/ Society Red/Rosepetal/Stormy Port/Wine Kiss/Meditation in Purple

I see a Gash in a Sugarplum.
It is an Amber Stain,
Like Satin and Gloss,
And tastes like Pink Ice.
A Wine Kiss. It is a Meditation in Purple.
More so than the Society Red Rosepetal
Floating through the Stormy Port.

Toast of New York/King Kong/Nicole/Mauve/Violets/ Tea

King Kong was the Toast of New York.
He and Nicole had a Mauve time, yes,
All Tea and Violets.

Captive/Del Rio/Cinnamon/Nude/Cabaret/Wine with Everything/Cinema Pink/No. 17/Champagne/Twig

In the pink cinema I feel like champagne
In seat Number 17
As I watch the captive lady,
Dolores Del Rio. She is like a twig
In a nude cabaret, Drinking
Cinnamon wine with everything.

Spice/Dr Pepper/Caramel/Chocolate/Boysenberry/ Diva/Piaf/Flirt

Dr Pepper thinks he's Chocolate,
Caramel think's he's Spice.
And you think you are a Boysenberry Diva,
Just like that Flirt named Piaf.

Vixen/Scarlett/Red Light/Wet Thunder/Kiss/Pearl
> The Vixen was Scarlett in the Red Light
> A mix of Wet Thunder, a Kiss, and a Pearl.

You can also make specific color poems and haiku. For example, you can make a Pink Poem, using just the colors of pink lipsticks.

Here is a purple and berry-colored poem:

Flaunt/Purple Haze/Captive/Violin/Phantom/Plague/ Deadly Nightshade
> The Violin player was a Phantom in the Purple Haze.
> The Plague Flaunts its Captive in the
> Deadly Nightshade.

You can make an Opalescent Poem, using opalescents, or a Full Color Wheel Poem. How about a Matte Poem? A Sheer Poem? The possibilities are endless.

SOME OF THE USES THAT POP CULTURE, ARCHITECTURE, ART, THE MOVIES, AND DREAM ANALYSIS HAVE FOUND FOR LIPSTICK

ARCHITECTURAL USES FOR A LIPSTICK IN THE TWENTIETH CENTURY:

🖌**LIPSTICK AS AN URBAN LANDSCAPE SKYLINE MARKER (BERLIN):** "Lipstick and Powder Box Building," part of a church damaged and reconstructed after World War II, is one of many structures in the city built to express Berlin's feelings toward the state of the world (for example, another sculpture near the Lipstick and Powder Box is the affectionately titled "Wet Meatball").

🖌 **LIPSTICK AS AN URBAN LANDSCAPE SKYLINE MARKER (NEW YORK CITY):** The "Lipstick Building," or as it is more conservatively called, "The 53rd and 3rd Building," as designed by Philip Johnson and John Burgee, got its name from the public who came to adore the bevelled skyscraper. The skyscraper, symbol of the twentieth-century, in the shape of another leading twentieth-century image, seemed a genius match.

POP CULTURE USES FOR A LIPSTICK—
THE COMIC BOOK:

🖌 Lipstick has been used well as armor by female superheros. Wonder Woman never goes out into action without her lipstick on. Comic book heroes in general are lipstick superstars. Most of these heroes were born around the time the beauty business took off, and thus incorporate the importance of putting on a new face to create a new persona of strength. For most superheroes, you can still see the same person beneath the mask—yes, except with the new face, it's them, only better. Bad guys usually use too much lipstick—kind of like Jezebel, where too much or bad makeup equals evil. The ultimate in too much lipstick being a symbol of evil can be found in Batman's Joker.

ART HISTORY USES FOR A LIPSTICK:

🖌 **LIPSTICK SURREALISM:** The surrealists got a kick out of isolating parts of the body and sending them off on their own. The increasingly popular image of the lipsticked mouth in popular culture, as well as the surrealist's obsession with the devouring woman, made the surrealist artist a type of lipstick junkie in his own right. They enjoyed taking the lips off of the face, and sending them off into new landscapes—thus giving the lipsticked mouth a whole new arsenal of meaning.

🖌 **SALVADOR DALI AND THE LIPSTICK:** The Mae West Sofa (also Saliva Sofa) a three-dimensional set of lips in shocking pink, shaped like Mae's mouth was a typical Salvador Dali lipstick masterpiece. He also created ads for his pal Elsa Schiaparelli, who had also entered the lipstick front, introducing her famous "Shocking Pink."

🖌 **ELSA SCHIAPARELLI AND THE LIPSTICK:** One part fashion designer, one part all-out surrealist, she created a suit that came with a mirror stitched into it so the wearer could use it to apply lipstick.

🖌 **MAN RAY AND THE LIPSTICK:** In the famous painting, "L'Observatoire" ("In the Hour of the Observatory—The Lovers"), a pair of red lipsticked lips, which look as if they've flown off a face, soar over a gloomy landscape with an observatory lurking in the background. According to Man Ray, the lips are the bodies of two lovers, pressed together, soaring in ecstacy. They are the lips of Lee Miller, Man Ray's ex-girlfriend in exile, whom he missed terribly when he created the work. As Man Ray wrote: "Your mouth becomes two bodies."

POP ART USES FOR A LIPSTICK: Pop artists featured lips as objects all by themselves, as if the painted lips alone were objects for consumption, just like a Brillo box, bottle of Coke, or a can of ravioli, were presented with a shiny brand-new surface and just-purchased gleam.

ANDY WARHOL AND LIPSTICK: Like many others who grew up in the Depression, Andy Warhol spent a good deal of his younger years gazing up at movie stars on the silver screen, fantasizing about their lives. Warhol gave movie star makeovers to the movie stars themselves in his paintings—Liza, Judy, Greta, Liz, and Ingrid were given even more fabulous and glamorous lipstick. Andy also paid an all-out tribute to lipstick with his book *Lips,* devoted entirely to the attainment of the perfectly painted mouth; and creating the Rolling Stones logo of the fat red Jaggerlike lips.

CLAES OLDENBURG AND LIPSTICK: "Lipstick (Ascending) on Caterpillar Tracks" is probably lipstick's most famous appearance as an art object. Erected at Yale University, the giant missile-shaped lipstick on a tank-shaped base inspired by caterpillar tractors mounted next to a World War I memorial quickly became a commentary on monuments, female versus male forms and war. Made from aluminum, steel, and wood, it was originally going to be an inflatable lipstick, to be blow up any time someone wanted to attract attention for a speech. They must have a thing about lipstick in New Haven. Yale is also the place the term "lipstick lesbian" originated.

LIPSTICK USES IN THE ART OF THE 1980s AND 1990s—THE LIPSTICK IS THE ART:

✒ **LIPSTICK URINALS:** Rachel Lachowicz parodies famous male works of art by redoing them in lipsticks (bought wholesale in five-gallon buckets). In "Red David," Michelangelo's torso is redone in red wax, in "Untitled (Lipstick Urinals)," Duchamp's urinals are recast in lipstick, and in "Blue Venus," a two-foot-long lipstick is strapped to a man's penis, which he then uses to draw.

✒ **LIPSTICK MENORAH:** For the Jewish Museum's exhibit "Too Jewish?", Cary Leibowitz and Rhonda Lieberman created "Chanel Hanukkah," which included a menorah made from a Chanel quilted clutch bag that had flame-red Chanel lipsticks placed on the top for candles. The lipsticks could then be screwed up or down to light or extinguish them.

✒ **"IS YOUR MAKEUP CRASHPROOF?"** In this exhibit, artist Sylvie Fleury presented a crashed car painted in lipstick color, and gigantic lipsticks covered in car paint.

✒ **LIPSTICK, CHOCOLATE, AND SPIT:** For Janine Antoni's "Diary," over 100 lipsticks were handmixed, then Antoni wore each separate one for over 100 separate daily activities. The lipstick remains were then put on display as one kind of recorded diary of her life. For "Gnaw," the artist gnawed at two 600-pound cubes of chocolate and lard for approximately three months, collecting the pieces she spit out as she went along. The chewed chocolate was molded into heart-shaped candy trays; the lard used as a base for 300 lipsticks. These nicely formed objects were placed in a department store–like glass case and erected opposite the two big gnawed-up cubes.

LIPSTICK DRESS by Janet Biggs—a triptych of three large-scale Cibachrome prints—was created by impaling 3,000 bullets of knockoff Chanel-red lipsticks on a dressmaker's mannequin and covering it with an aggressive multitude of strap-ons, wherein the image of lipstick becomes armor.

MOVIE STAR USES FOR LIPSTICK:

"Adding sound to movies would be like putting lipstick on the Venus de Milo."

— MARY PICKFORD

For every ten movies you'll watch, most likely eight of them have lipstick in the cast. My favorite movie moment where lipstick appears as an actor is in *The Breakfast Club,* where Molly Ringwald shows her talent at putting on lipstick with her breasts. Two other great lipstick acting jobs (where it demonstrates the Madness Theory of Lipstick) are *Sunset Boulevard,* and *What Ever Happened to Baby Jane?*

USING LIPSTICKS TO MARKET MOVIES:

🖋 Lorac's "Long Kiss" was made for Geena Davis to wear in *The Long Kiss Goodnight.* Urban Decay, in conjunction with the premiere of the black comic hostage movie *A Life Less Ordinary,* ran a contest for a new urban lipstick color. The winner created "Lottery"—the contestant took a penny and a dime, placed them side by side, and included the directions to take the two and swirl them together for the color. Urban Decay also created "The Wedding Singer" lipstick for Drew Barrymore in a film by the same name (the lipstick's been renamed "Crime"). "007 Lipstick" by YSL timed its launch to coordinate with the fall release of the James Bond movie *Goldeneye.*

And finally . . .

LIPSTICK AS A SYMBOL IN FREUDIAN (AND OTHER) DREAM ANALYSIS:

🖋 If surrealism is a playground for the unconscious, does that mean that lipstick in dreams is significant? In *Mary Summer Rain's Guide to Dream*

Symbols, dreaming of lipstick "will denote inner personality traits." The color of the lipstick—whether it's brown or red or maroon—will clue you in further. In *The Dreamer's Dictionary,* by Lady Stearn, dreaming of buying makeup is a sign of fortune, unless you're a guy buying women's stuff—then it's a warning of business reverses due to loss of reputation. According to the book by the dream master Orion, *Dreams: Hidden Meaning and Secrets,* "To dream that you see a woman using lipstick in a public place is a portent of defeat in a struggle. You will be the butt of a practical joke if you dream of seeing a man use lipstick." Does that mean that the lips flying over the observatory in Man Ray's painting are coming to tell you that you're about to lose your job? Or worse, that you're about to sit on a whoopee cushion?

CHAPTER ELEVEN

LIPSTICK 2000

In 1968, Mary Quant announced that she wanted to create pills you'd take in the morning to get the desired rosy glow, to stimulate your lips, and to make your eyelashes grow. In *Beyond the Looking Glass*, Kathrin Perutz writes that Clairol was predicting a pill that would change hair color, and makeup that was actually built into cleansing cream. Perutz also cites a chief chemist at Helena Rubinstein predicting injections to change hair color, plastic skin that you'd be able to buy to reshape your face, and a fragrance pill to replace perfume.

But I don't think lipstick does well when it comes to

futuristic advances. I think lipstick likes being simple, primitive, pure. It likes being exactly what it is. Most major technological attempts at redoing lipstick have been failures. It's like the orgasm pill that scientists keep talking about. Sorry, it can't replace the real thing.

Same thing with lipstick. The purposes lipstick served a few thousand years ago will most likely be those that are served in the future.

The more I think about my own lipstick addiction, and the more lipstick addicts talk, I'm always more convinced of one thing: The Girl Can't Help It.

And we need that red. We need it in the same way we need water. Our bodies are made up of so much red fluid, I think that we crave it. As far as the history of body paint is concerned, red goes back the farthest, and is mentioned more often than any other color. Recently dug up Cro-Magnon and Neanderthal graves have revealed evidence of red ocher with mallet or brushlike sticks nearby that indicate the pigments were drawn or tattooed onto the body. The pleasingly plump Venus of Willendorf, the prehistoric female object discovered in Austria, had red ocher traces scribbled on her body. Then there was the 5,000-year-old Ice Age man who was uncovered in the Italian Alps. Again, the detectives found a red-tattooed upper torso. And those excavational wizards, the Leakeys, dug up artifacts of the 24,000 B.C. cave dwellers, and again found the same evidence: Red Ocher Was Here.

The grunting dudes with club in hand continue to be unearthed, and always with brand-new arrows pointing to the suspicion of red body paint. And where there's red body paint, you know there's lipstick. Give it a few years, and they'll excavate a dinosaur wearing lipstick.

Until that day comes (and I'm not convinced it won't), may that primal itch for the glossy red wax keep you feeling happy, colorful, orally sound, clothed, protected from the demons, ready to do battle, and filled with magic. And may your primordial hunt bring you to that pot of gold (or red dye) at the end of the rainbow: the perfect lip-stick.

BIBLIOGRAPHY

Ackerman, Diane. *A Natural History of Love*. New York: Random House, 1994.

Ackerman, Diane. *A Natural History of the Senses*. New York: Vintage/Random House, 1990.

Allen, Margaret. *Selling Dreams: Inside the Beauty Business*. New York: Simon and Schuster, 1981.

Angeloglou, Maggie. *A History of Make-up*. New York: Macmillan Press, 1970.

Arpel, Adrien. *Adrien Arpel's 851 Fast Beauty Fixes and Facts*. New York: G. P. Putnam's Sons, 1985.

Atkinson, George William. *Perfumes and Their Preparations*. New York: Norman W. Henley and Co., 1892.

Aucoin, Kevyn. *The Art of Makeup*. New York: HarperCollins, 1994.

Aucoin, Kevyn. *Making Faces*. Boston: Little Brown, 1997.

Ayer, Harriet Hubbard. *Harriet Hubbard Ayer's Book: A Complete and Authentic Treatise on the Laws of Health and Beauty*. New York: Reprinted by Arno Press and Quadrangle/The New York Times Book Co., 1974.

Baker, Nancy C. *The Beauty Trap: Exploring Woman's Greatest Obsession*. New York: Franklin Watts, 1984.

Baldwin, Neil. *Man Ray: American Artist*. New York: Clarkson Potter, 1988.

Bandy, Way. *Designing Your Face*. New York: Random House, 1977.

Bandy, Way. *Styling Your Face*. New York: Random House, 1981.

Barnes, E. W. *The Lady of Fashion: The Life and Theater of Anna Cora Mowatt*. New York: Scribners, 1954.

Barnhart, David K. and Metcalf, Allan A. *America: In So Many Words*. New York: Houghton Mifflin, 1977.

Basten, Fred E. *Max Factor's Hollywood: Glamour—Movies—Make-Up*. Los Angeles, CA: General Publishing Group, 1995.

Batterby, Michael and Ariane. *Fashion: The Mirror of History*. Greenwich House/Crown, 1982.

Begoun, Paula. *The Beauty Bible*. Seattle, WA: Beginning Press, 1997.

Begoun, Paula. *Blue Eyeshadow Should Still Be Illegal*. Seattle, WA: Beginning Press, 1988.

Begoun, Paula. *Don't Go to the Cosmetics Counter Without Me.* Seattle, WA: Beginning Press, 1997.

Besserman, Lujo. *The Oldest Profession: A History of Prostitution.* Germany: 1965. Reprinted by Dorset Press, New York, 1993.

Brown, Bobbi and Iverson, Annemarie. *Bobbi Brown Beauty.* New York: HarperCollins, 1997.

Brown, Helen Gurley, Editor/*Cosmopolitan* magazine. *The Cosmo Girl's Guide to the New Etiquette.* New York: Cosmopolitan Books, 1961.

Brumberg, Elaine. *Save Your Money, Save Your Face.* New York: Facts on File, 1986.

Brusatin, Manlio. *A History of Colors.* Originally published 1983 by Guilio Einaudi editore s.p.a., Torino. Translated and reissued by Shambhala Publications, Boston and London, 1991.

Bushby, Robert. *Cosmetics and How to Make Them.* London: Sir Isaac Pitman and Sons, 1947.

Butterick Publishing. *Beauty: It's Attainment and Preservation.* New York: Butterick, 1890.

Byrne, Robert. *1,911 Best Things Anybody Ever Said.* Fawcett Columbine/Ballantine, 1988.

Cane, William. *The Art of Kissing.* New York: St. Martin's Press, 1995.

Carpenter, Deb. *Nature's Beauty Kit: Cosmetic Recipes You Can Make at Home.* Golden, Co.: Fulervon Publishing, 1995.

Cirlot, J. E. *A Dictionary of Symbols.* Routledge and Kegan Paul, 1971.

Cohn, David L. *The Good Old Days: A History of American Morals and Manners as Seen Through the Sears Roebuck Catalogs.* New York: Simon and Schuster, 1940. Reprinted 1976 by Arno Press.

Cole, Lorin. *The Complete Book of Make-Up.* Stamford, CT: Longmeadow Press, 1995.

Collins, Joan. *Health, Youth and Happiness: My Secrets.* New York: Putnam, 1995.

Cooley, Arnold J. *The Toilet in Ancient and Modern Times.* London: R. Hardwick, 1886. Reprinted by Burt Franklin, NY, 1970.

Corson, Richard. *Fashions in Makeup from Ancient to Modern Times.* New York: Universe Books, 1972.

Cox, Janice. *Natural Beauty at Home.* New York: Owl Books, 1995.

Cox, Janice. *Natural Beauty for All Seasons.* New York: Owl Books, 1996.

Crawford, Joan. *My Way of Life*. New York: Simon and Schuster, 1971.

Craze, Richard. *The Spice Companion: The Culinary, Cosmetic, and Medicinal Uses of Spices*. People's Medical Society, 1997.

Crum, J. Howard. *Beauty and Health*. New York: The World Publishing Co., 1943.

Dare, Frances. *Lovely Ladies: The Art of Being a Woman*. New York: Doubleday, 1929.

de Castelbajac, Kate. *The Face of the Century: 100 Years of Makeup and Style*. New York: Rizzoli Press, 1995.

de Montaigne, Michel. *Essays*. Translated by J. M. Cohen. New York: Penguin Books. Translation originally published 1958.

Donnan, Marcia. *Cosmetics in the Kitchen*. New York: Holt, Rinehart and Winston, 1972.

Duby, Georges, Editor. *A History of Private Life*. Belknap Press/Harvard University Press, 1988.

Ettinger, Rosanne. *Compacts and Smoking Accessories*. West Chester, PA: Schiffer Publishing, 1991.

Everett, Felicity. *Makeup*. London: Usborne Publishing, London, 1986.

Fabe, Maxene. *Beauty Millionaire: The Life of Helena Rubinstein*. New York: Thomas Y. Crowell Co., 1972.

Falconi, Dina. *Earthly Bodies and Heavenly Hair*. Woodstock, NY: Cere Press, 1998.

Fisher, Patricia, Editor. *Age Erasers for Women*. Rodale Press, 1994.

Francis, Mark and King, Margery, Editors. *The Warhol Look: Glamour, Style, Fashion*. Boston/New York: Bulfinch Press/Little Brown, 1997.

Gair, Angela. *Artist's Manual: A Complete Guide to Painting and Drawing Materials and Techniques*. San Francisco, CA: Chronicle Books, 1995.

Gernsheim, Alison. *Victorian and Edwardian Fashion*. New York: Dover, 1982.

Gerson, Roselyn. *Vintage Ladies' Compacts*. Paducah, KY: Collector Books, 1996.

Glamour magazine, Editors of. *Glamour's Beauty Book*. New York: Simon and Schuster, 1957.

Goodrum and Dalrymple. *Advertising in America: The First 200 Years*. New York: Abrams, 1990.

Gunn, Fenja. *The Artificial Face*. New York: Hippocrene Books, 1973.

Hampton, Aubrey. *What's in Your Cosmetics?: A Complete Consumer's Guide to Natural and Synthetic Ingredients.* Tucson, AZ: Odonian Press, 1995.

Harriman, Mrs. Oliver. *Mrs. Oliver Harriman's Book of Etiquette.* New York: Greenberg Publishers, 1942.

Heymann, C. David. *Liz: An Intimate Biography of Elizabeth Taylor.* Ontario: Citidel Stars/Carol Publishing, 1995.

Hollander, Anne. *Seeing Through Clothes.* New York: Viking Press, 1975.

Irons, Diane. *The World's Best-Kept Beauty Secrets.* Naperville, IL: Sourcebooks, 1997.

Israel, Lee. *Estee Lauder: Beyond the Magic.* New York: Macmillan, 1985.

James, Peter and Thorpe, Nick. *Ancient Inventions.* New York: Ballantine Books, 1994.

Keenan, Brigid. *The Women We Wanted to Look Like.* New York: St. Martin's Press, 1977.

Kellar, Casey. *The Natural Beauty and Bath Book.* Lark Books, 1997.

Kennett, Frances. *The Collectors Book of Fashion.* New York: Crown Publishers, 1993.

Kowalckik, Claire and Hylton, William H., Editors. *Rodale's Illustrated Encyclopedia of Herbs.* Emmaus, PA: Rodale Press, 1987.

Kramer, Samuel Noah. *History Begins at Sumer: 39 Firsts in Recorded History.* University of Pennsylvania Press, 1981.

Krochmal, Connie. *A Guide to Natural Cosmetics.* New York: Quadrangle/New York Times Books, 1973.

La Rue, ChiChi. *Making It Big: Sex Stars, Porn Films, and Me.* Los Angeles, CA: Alyson Books, 1997.

Lappe, Marc. *The Body's Edge: Our Cultural Obsession With Skin.* New York: Henry Holt and Company, 1996.

Laubner, Ellie. *Fashions of the Roaring '20s.* Atglen, PA: Schiffer Publishing Ltd., 1996.

Lauder, Estèe. *Estèe: A Success Story.* New York: Random House, 1985.

Liggett, John. *The Human Face.* New York: Stein and Day, 1974.

Loren, Sophia. *Women and Beauty.* New York: William Morrow, 1984.

Lurie, Alison. *The Language of Clothes.* New York: Random House, 1981.

Lipovetsky, Gilles. *The Empire of Fashion: Dressing Modern Democracy.* Princeton University Press, 1994.

Livingstone, Marco. *Pop Art: A Continuing History.* New York: Harry N. Abrams, 1990.

Macrone, Michael. *Brush Up Your Bible!* New York: Cader Books/ HarperCollins Publishers, 1993.

Martin, Richard. *Fashion and Surrealism.* New York: Rizzoli, 1987.

Mason, Linda. *Linda Mason's Sun-Sign Makeovers.* New York: Farrar Strauss & Giroux, 1985.

McDonough, Everett G. *The Truth About Cosmetics.* Published by The Drug and Cosmetic Industry, 1937.

McLeod, Edyth Thornton. *Beauty After Forty.* Chicago/New York: Ziff-Davis Publishing, 1949.

Messner, Tammy Faye [Bakker]. *Tammy: Telling It My Way.* New York: Villard, 1996.

Meyer, Carolyn. *Being Beautiful: The Story of Cosmetics From Ancient Art to Modern Science.* New York: William Morrow, 1977.

Miles, Christopher, and Norwich, John Julius. *Love in the Ancient World.* New York: St. Martin's Press, 1998.

Morris, Christopher. *The Tudors.* London: B. T. Batsford Ltd., 1955.

Morris, Desmond. *Intimate Behavior.* New York: Bantam, 1971.

Morris, Edwin T. *Fragrance: The Story of Perfume from Cleopatra to Chanel.* New York: Charles Scribner's Sons, 1984.

Mueller, Laura M. *Collector's Encyclopedia of Compacts: Carryalls and Face Powder Boxes* (Volumes I and II). Paducah: Collector Books, 1996, 1997.

Muramto, Naboru. *Healing Ourselves.* New York: Swan House Publishing/Avon Books, 1973.

Orion. *Dreams: Hidden Meaning and Secrets.* New York: Prentice Hall, 1987.

Oxford University Press. *Oxford Dictionary of Quotations.* Oxford, England: Oxford University Press, 1981.

Panati, Charles. *Panati's Extraordinary Origins of Everyday Things.* New York: Harper & Row, 1987.

Panati, Charles. *Sexy Origins and Intimate Things.* New York: Penguin Books, 1998.

Paris, Barry. *Louise Brooks.* New York: Alfred A. Knopf, 1989.

Peiss, Kathy. *Hope in a Jar: The Making of America's Beauty Culture.* New York: Metropolitan Books/Henry Holt and Company, 1998.

Perella, Nicholas J. *The Kiss Sacred and Profane: An Interpretive History of Kiss Symbolism and Related Religious-Erotic Themes.* Berkeley/Los Angeles: University of California Press, 1969.

Perutz, Kathrin. *Beyond the Looking Glass: America's Beauty Culture.* New York: William Morrow, 1970.

Peter, Dr. Laurence J. *Peter's Quotations: Ideas for Our Time*. New York: William Morrow, 1997.

Powell, Jillian. *Body Decoration* (Traditions Around the World series). New York: Thomas Learning, 1995.

Power, Vicki. *Vanity: A Very Peculiar History*. New York: Franklin Watts, 1995.

Powers, John Robert. *The Powers Girl*. New York: Dutton, 1941.

Raichur, Pratima. *Absolute Beauty*. New York: HarperCollins, 1997.

Rain, Mary Summer and Greystone, Alex. *Mary Summer Rain's Guide to Dream Symbols*. Charlottesville, VA: Hampton Road Publishing, 1996.

Roach, Mary Ellen and Eicher, Joanne Bubolz. *Dress, Adornment, and the Social Order*. New York: John Wiley and Sons, 1965.

Robinson, Jeffrey. *Bardot: An Intimate Portrait*. New York: Donald I. Fine Books, 1994.

Robinson, Julian. *Body Packaging: A Guide to Human Sexual Display*. Los Angeles: Elysium Growth Press.

Robinson, Julian. *The Quest for Human Beauty*. New York/London: W. W. Norton and Company, 1998.

Robinson, Lady Stearn and Tom Corbett. *The Dreamer's Dictionary*. New York: Warner Books, 1974.

Rubinstein, Helena. *My Life for Beauty*. New York: Simon and Schuster, 1964.

Rubinstein, Ruth P. *Dress Codes: Meanings and Messages in American Culture*. Boulder, CO: Westview Press, 1995.

Sachs, Melanie. *Ayurvedic Beauty Care*. Twin Lakes, WI: Lotus Press, 1994.

Safire, William and Safir, Leonard, Editors. *Words of Wisdom: More Good Advice*. New York: Fireside/Simon and Schuster, 1989.

Scheman, Andrew, M.D. and Severson, David L. *Cosmetics Buying Guide*. Yonkers, New York: Consumer Reports Books, 1993.

Schnurnberger, Lynn. *Let There Be Clothes*. New York: Workman Publishing, 1991.

Schultz, Christine and the Editors of The Old Farmer's Almanac. *The Book of Love*. New York: Villard/Random House/Yankee Publishing, 1996.

Shalleck, Jamie. *Masks*. New York: Viking Press, 1973.

Shuker, Nancy. *Elizabeth Arden: Cosmetics Entrepreneur*. Englewood Cliffs, NY: Silver Burdett Press (The American Dream Series), 1989.

Stabile, Toni. *Everything You Want to Know about Cosmetics*. New York: Dodd, Mead and Company, 1984.

Stacey, Sarah and Fairley, Josephine. *The Beauty Bible*. Woodstock, New York: Overlook Press, 1996.

Stephens, Autumn. *Wild Words from Wild Women*. Berkeley, CA: Conari Press, 1993.

Swinfield, Rosemarie. *Stage Makeup: Step-by-Step*. Cincinnati, OH: Betterway Books, 1994.

Theroux, Alexander. *The Primary Colors*. New York: Henry Holt, 1994.

Theroux, Alexander. *The Secondary Colors*. New York: Henry Holt, 1996.

Tobias, Andrew. *Fire and Ice: The Story of Charles Revson—The Man Who Built the Revlon Empire*. New York: William Morrow, 1976.

Tortora, Phyllis and Eubank, Keith. *Survey of Historic Costume*. New York: Fairchild Publications, 1994.

Traven, Beatrice. *The Complete Book of Natural Cosmetics*. New York: Simon and Schuster, 1974.

Tyldesley, Joyce. *Daughters of Isis: Women of Ancient Egypt*. New York/London: Penguin Books, 1994.

Ultra Violet (Isabelle Dufresne). *Famous for 15 Minutes: My Years with Andy Warhol*. New York: Harcourt Brace Jovanovich, 1988.

Vail, Gilbert. *A History of Cosmetics in America*. New York: The Toilet Goods Association, 1947.

Vera, Veronica. *Miss Vera's Finishing School for Boys Who Want to Be Girls*. New York: Doubleday, 1997.

Walker, Barbara G. *The Woman's Dictionary of Symbols and Sacred Objects*. HarperSanFrancisco/a Division of HarperCollins, 1988.

Walker, Barbara G. *The Woman's Encyclopedia of Myths and Secrets*. HarperSanFrancisco/a Division of HarperCollins, 1983.

Warhol, Andy. *THE Philosophy of Andy Warhol (From A to B and Back Again)*. New York: Harcourt Brace Jovanovich, 1975.

Winter, Ruth. *A Consumer's Dictionary of Cosmetic Ingredients*. New York: Three Rivers Press/Crown, 1994.

Woods, Tim and Dicks, Ian. *What They Don't Teach You about History*. London: Simon and Schuster, 1990.

VIDEO REFERENCES:

Beauty Queens—*Elizabeth Arden, Helena Rubinstein, Estèe Lauder* (Public Media Video)

Elizabeth R (BBC; starring Glenda Jackson)

25 x 5: The Continuing Adventures of the Rolling Stones (CBS Video)

PERIODICALS AND CATALOGS:

American Magazines: *Allure, Cosmetics and Toiletries* (January 1978), *Cosmopolitan, Glamour, Good Housekeeping, Harper's Bazaar, In Style, Jane, Jump, Ladies Home Journal, Mademoiselle, Marie-Claire, Mirabella, Movie, The New York Times Magazine, The New Yorker, People, Photoplay, Sassy, Sears and Roebuck Catalog, Seventeen, Teen People, Time Out New York, Vogue, W, Women's Wear Daily, YM.*

UK Magazines: *B, The Face, Jackie, Sugar, Woman's Journal* (April 1998), *British Vogue, Frank.*

International Magazines: *Australian Vogue, Italian Vogue, German Vogue, French Vogue, Elle, Cutie* (Japan), *Russian Vogue, Donna, Flare* (Canada), *Marie Claire.*

NOTES

CHAPTER ONE: A BRIEF HISTORY OF LIPSTICK

1. Kramer, Samuel Noah. *History Begins at Sumer: 39 Firsts in Recorded History*. University of Pennsylvania Press, 1981.

2. Basten, Fred E. *Max Factor's Hollywood: Glamour—Movies—Make-Up*. Los Angeles, CA: General Publishing Group, 1995.

3. *Beauty Queens: Volume Two—Elizabeth Arden*. Public Media Video.

CHAPTER TWO: LIPSTICK FOR BEGINNERS

1. Morris, Desmond. *Intimate Behavior*. New York: Bantam, 1971.

2. Brown, Bobbi and Iverson, Annemarie. *Bobbi Brown Beauty*. New York: HarperCollins, 1997. Page 125.

3. Perutz, Kathrin. *Beyond the Looking Glass: America's Beauty Culture*. New York: William Morrow, 1970. (for Bill Mandel quote)

4. Ann Richardson, as quoted on "CBS Sunday Morning", Oct. 25, 1992 while discussing a Republican candidate for the presidency and that party's attempt to make him more appealing.

5. Lauder, Estèe. *Estèe: A Success Story*. New York: Random House, 1985.

Other Primary References for This Chapter:

Lappe, Marc. *The Body's Edge: Our Cultural Obsession With Skin*. New York: Henry Holt and Company, 1996.

CHAPTER THREE: LIPSTICK FREUD

1. Brown, Bobbi and Iverson, Annemarie. *Bobbi Brown Beauty*, p. 129.

CHAPTER FOUR: LIPSTICK FACT AND FICTION

1. Peiss, Kathy. *Hope in a Jar. The Making of America's Beauty Culture.* New York: Metropolitan Books/Henry Holt and Company, 1998.

Other Primary References for This Chapter:

de Castelbajac, Kate. *The Face of the Century: 100 Years of Makeup and Style.* New York: Rizzoli Press, 1995.

James, Peter and Thorpe, Nick. *Ancient Inventions.* New York: Ballantine Books, 1994.

Macrone, Michael. *Brush Up Your Bible!* New York: Cader Books/HarperCollins, 1993.

Panati, Charles. *Panati's Extraordinary Origins of Everyday Things.* New York: Harper & Row, 1987.

CHAPTER FIVE: HOW TO GROW A LIPSTICK

1. Information on ingredients was taken primarily from two sources: *What's in Your Cosmetics?* by Aubrey Hampton. Tucson, AZ: Odonian Press, 1995, and *A Consumer's Dictionary of Cosmetic Ingredients,* by Ruth Winter, M.S., New York: Three Rivers Press/Crown, 1994.

2. Peter, Laurence J. *Peter's Quotations: Ideas for Our Time,* New York: William Morrow, 1997. Page 531.

3. Ibid. Page 532.

4. Stephens, Autumn. *Wild Words from Wild Women,* Berkeley, CA: Conari Press, 1993. Page 15.

5. Walker, Barbara G. *The Woman's Encyclopedia of Myths and Secrets.* Harper San Francisco/Harper Collins. 1983.

6. de Montaigne, Michel. *Essays.* New York: Penguin Books. From the essay "On Smells." Page 135.

7. *Harpers Bazaar,* September 1995. Page 232.

CHAPTER SIX: HOW TO BUY A LIPSTICK

1. Tobias, Andrew. *Fire and Ice: The Story of Charles Revson— The Man Who Built the Revlon Empire.* New York: William Morrow, 1976. Page 107.

2.   "25 × 5: The Continuing Adventures of The Rolling Stones" (CBS Music Video Enterprises). Excerpted from an interview with Keith Richards.

3.   Begoun, Paula. *Don't Go to the Cosmetics Counter Without Me.* Seattle, WA: Beginning Press, 1997. Pages 20–22.

4.   Loren, Sophia. *Women and Beauty.* New York: William Morrow, 1984.

5.   Collins, Joan. *Health, Youth and Happiness: My Secrets.* New York: Putnam, 1995.

CHAPTER SEVEN: HOUDINI AND MERLIN'S LIPSTICK AND OTHER TRICKS OF THE TRADE

1.   La Rue, ChiChi. *Making It Big: Sex Stars, Porn Films, and Me.* Los Angeles, CA: Alyson Books, 1997. Page 223.

2.   Brown, Bobbi and Iverson, Annemarie. *Bobbi Brown Beauty.* Page 125.

3.   *Vogue* magazine, December 1997. "A Woman of Substance." Page 304.

4.   Warhol, Andy. *THE Philosophy of Andy Warhol (from A to B and Back Again),* New York: Harcourt Brace Jovanovich, 1975. Page 64.

5.   *The Concise Oxford Dictionary of Quotations.* Oxford, England: Oxford University Press, Page 238.

6.   Peter, Dr. Laurence J. *Peter's Quotations: Ideas for Our Time.* Page 503.

7.   Vera, Veronica. *Miss Vera's Finishing School for Boys Who Want to Be Girls.* New York: Doubleday, 1997. Page 95.

8.   Arpel, Adrien. *Adrien Arpel's 851 Fast Beauty Fixes and Facts.* New York: G. P. Putnam's Sons, 1985. Page 119.

9.   Stephens, Autumn. *Wild Words from Wild Women.* Page 15.

10.   Brown, Bobbi and Iverson, Annemarie. *Bobbi Brown Beauty.* Page 125.

11.   Peri Gilpin quote from a 1997 *People* magazine spotlight article on red lipstick.

12.   *Harper's Bazaar,* March 1998 "How To Wear a Serious Lipstick," page 234 (for tips from Kevyn Aucoin).

13. Peter, Dr. Laurence J. *Peter's Quotations: Ideas for Our Time*. Page 297.

14. Ovid. *The Art of Love*.

15. Cunningham, Laura. "Why I Wear My False Eyelashes to Bed." *The Cosmo Girl's Guide to The New Etiquette*. Editor: Helen Gurley Brown. New York: Cosmopolitan Books, 1961.

Other Primary References for This Chapter:

Crawford, Joan. *My Way of Life*. New York: Simon and Schuster, 1971 (all quotes attributed to Ms. Crawford were obtained from this book).

Bandy, Way. *Designing Your Face*. New York: Random House, 1977.

Bandy, Way. *Styling Your Face*. New York: Random House, 1981.

(All tips and techniques attributed to Way Bandy were taken from these two books.)

CHAPTER NINE: THE TIME TRAVELER'S LIPSTICK

Primary References for This Chapter:

Angeloglou, Maggie. *A History of Make-up*. New York: Macmillan Press, 1970.

Corson, Richard. *Fashions in Makeup From Ancient to Modern Times*. New York: Universe Books, 1972.

Gunn, Fenja. *The Artificial Face*. New York: Hippocrene Books, 1973.

Shalleck, Jamie. *Masks*. New York: Viking Press, 1973.

ACKNOWLEDGMENTS

FOR CONTINUOUS ASSISTANCE: PARTICULAR THANKS TO: Neeti Madan and Jennifer Enderlin. Thanks also to Charlotte Sheedy, David Forrer, Ludger Krane, Stephane Houy-Towner at The Costume Institute, Metropolitan Museum of Art; Diane Hughes, Inessa Sikiric, Dee Dee Zobian, Marsha Mihok, Catherine Ortiz, and the family: Raya, Suzy, Stewart, Tammy and Alina.

AT THE COSMETIC COMPANIES, THANKS TO THE FOLLOWING INDIVIDUALS FOR THEIR INTERVIEWS AND INFORMATION: Jean Danielson and Beth Puccinelli at BeneFit; Frank Toskan, Jill Amateo, and Joanne Lupis at M•A•C; François Nars and Kate Sullivan at NARS; Lisa Silvera and Martina Arfwidson at FACE Stockholm; Jeanine Lobell and Raj Singh at Stila; Roja Dove and Kara Green at Guerlain; Laura Lee at Shu Uemura; Carol Shaw at Lorac; Julie Leong and Kimberly Forrest at Prescriptives; Brooke Hargrove at Uni; Tish and Snooky Bellomo and Ken West at Manic Panic; Matthew Van Leeuwin at InBeauty; Cristina Bornstein at Tony & Tina; Cristina Carlino and Beth Berdofe at Philosophy; Poppy King and Linda Falcone at Poppy; Wende Zomnir at Urban Decay; Diego Dalla Palma; Betsy Olum, and Gilles Masse at Diego Dalla Palma; Russell Pfluger at English Ideas; Shannon Cooney at Clinique, R. Lowe at Bobbi Brown, Anna Bayle; Alchemy Cosmetics/Hard Candy.

FOR TECHNICAL, RESOURCE, AND FINE ARTS INTERVIEWS AND INFORMATION, THANKS TO: The technical and chemistry-related assistance of Paul Thau; the Fashion Institute of Technology/State University of New York; the artists Janet Biggs and Cary Leibowitz; Shoshanah Wayne Gallery; Postmasters Gallery; The Jewish Museum; The Whitney Museum of American Art; Kevin Reardon; and Veronica Vera at Miss Vera's Finishing School for Boys Who Want to Be Girls.

AND TO THE MANY PEOPLE WHO SHARED THEIR LIPSTICK STORIES, CONFESSIONS, AND TUBES OF LIPSTICK WITHOUT SHAME, THANKS PARTICULARLY TO: Megg Accordino, Wanda Baedekker, Mary Blake, Harriet Broadwin, Harriett Carracola, Carl, Allison Carr, Joyce Caruso, Michael Caruso, Valerie Cauley, Karen and Wanda Chamberlain, Angela Cheng, Stephanie Cheng, Willa Clinton, Colin, Kristin Gehring, Fran and Abe Gilman, Lizette Gonzales, Ruth Gottesman, Juliette Gray, Beverly Martin-Haines, Beverly Hemingway, Doris Hirsh, Shari Hurl, Laura Issler, Betty Jones, Julie Delia-Jones, Peggy Krementz, Evelyn Leonotti, Allan Margolies, Julie and Pete Opdyke, Katie Figueroa-Russell and her mom Suzy, Annette Sacks, Judith Speigel, Irene Tejeratchi, Betty Thomas, Ruthie Thomas, Annette Toomey, Richard Waltman, Yetta, Kevin Zilber; Harold, Bob, and Desiree; the students of K-106 at the Lower Lab School, PS 198, New York; the kind Willa Clinton, and friends at Warner Bros.